Introduction to Public Liability Policies

J P P Shaw
ACII, FCILA

Series editor: R M Walmsley

Croner Publications Ltd
Croner House
London Road
Kingston upon Thames
Surrey KT2 6SR
Telephone: 081-547 3333

Copyright © 1990 J P P Shaw
First published 1990

Published by
Croner Publications Ltd,
Croner House,
London Road,
Kingston upon Thames,
Surrey KT2 6SR
Telephone 081-547 3333

All rights reserved
No part of this publication may be reproduced,
stored in a retrieval system, or transmitted in any form or by
any means, electronic, mechanical, photocopying, recording,
or otherwise
without prior permission of
Croner Publications Ltd.

While every care has been taken
in the writing and editing of this book,
readers should be aware that only Acts of Parliament
and Statutory Instruments have the force of law,
and that only the courts can authoritatively
interpret the law.

British Library Cataloguing in Publication Data
Shaw, J. P. P.
An introduction to public liability policies.
1. Great Britain. Liability insurance
I. Title
368.500941

ISBN 1-85452-066-0

Typeset by Phoenix Photosetting, Chatham, Kent.
Printed by Whitstable Litho, Whitstable, Kent.

Introduction to Public Liability Policies

Contents

Series preface		vii
Introduction		ix
Chapter 1	Legal principles – summary of policy	1
Chapter 2	The recital clause	9
Chapter 3	The operative clause	19
Chapter 4	The proviso clause	35
Chapter 5	Exceptions – risks covered by other policies	41
Chapter 6	Exceptions – risks covered by other policies (continued) – product liability and professional indemnity insurance	57
Chapter 7	Exceptions – risks outside scope of the policy – uninsurable risks – excess clause	67
Chapter 8	Policy conditions	73
Chapter 9	Extensions to basic policy cover	89
Appendix A	Public liability policy	95
Appendix B	Sun Alliance Insurance Group liability insurance proposal	101

Appendix C	Sun Alliance Insurance Group liability policy	111
Appendix D	Colonia Insurance Company (UK) Limited liability policy	125
Appendix E	Association of British Insurers – Statement of General Insurance Practice	137
Appendix F	List of cases	141
Appendix G	Précis of cases	143
Index		173

Series preface

The day to day practice of insurance involves making decisions in relation to the interpretation of contract documents.

It is a practical job concerned with real problems for real people, and the books in this series are primarily intended to give essential basic information to insurance and professional students which will enable them to understand the principles involved in their work.

In addition, people insured in a private capacity and officials of insured companies need to understand those principles underlying the contracts into which they have entered. Thus this series should also be of value to them, both in the negotiation stage of arranging insurance cover and later when questions arise in relation to a claim.

The various authors are engaged in the claims field and thus the texts are based on practical experience.

R M Walmsley
Birmingham
July 1989

Introduction

One of the main purposes of insurance is to allow people to carry on their business or private affairs in the knowledge that, should they suffer loss or damage to their property or incur a liability to pay damages to a third party, their insurer will bear the expense involved: they will be indemnified. This is particularly important in the context of third party liabilities where the financial consequences of an accident could be well beyond the means of the person or company responsible. The highest award for damages for personal injury at the time of writing is £1,200,000 (*Harrop v Fernandez* (1989)). Claims and awards for damages resulting from pollution incidents or professional negligence are far in excess of this figure.

We are all, therefore, at risk of incurring liabilities which could not be met without insurance, and policyholders pay premiums into a fund from which claims are met. Insurers calculate premium rates by reference to previous claims experience, so that those engaged in activities giving the highest risk, whether by frequency or potential size of claims, pay the highest premiums.

Many accidental events are potential claims under public liability policies although they may not appear to be so at first sight. Most accidents have a cause and should this be attributable to fault or breach of a legal duty by any party, that party would probably incur a liability for which the public liability policy may provide an indemnity. Naturally such a policy is subject to certain conditions and exclusions, a consideration of which will be the subject of the major part of this book.

A number of cases are referred to in the text and appendices to illustrate important points or to assist the reader in understanding developments in the law as they effect the public liability policy. Some of these cases, in particular those that are of fundamental importance to the law of insurance, also appear in other books in this series. It is emphasised, however, that there is no substitute for reading the full reports and judgements of those cases and any others dealing with the same topic. Case report references are therefore given in Appendix C. As series editor, R M Walmsey has read the script and made various suggestions to clarify certain points. Nevertheless the opinion and interpretations as they appear in the text remain my responsibility.

I am grateful to the Association of British Insurers for their permission to reproduce the Statement of General Insurance Practice and must also record my thanks to Sun Alliance International Insurance Group and Colonia Insurance (UK) Limited for permission to reproduce proposal forms and policy documents.

CHAPTER 1

Legal principles – summary of policy

An insurance policy is evidence of a contract between the insurer and the policyholder, and is therefore subject to the principles of contract law. Without going into a detailed consideration of that area of the law, a contract can briefly be described as an agreement and an intention to create a legal relationship between the parties involved. The essential elements of a contract are:

(a) offer and acceptance;
(b) an intention to create legal relationships;
(c) consideration (unless the contract is under seal);
(d) the parties must have the capacity to contract;
(e) there must be consent between the parties to the contract terms;
(f) it must be legal and capable of performance.

The absence of one or more of these will make the contract void, voidable or unenforceable.

It is the intention of this book to analyse a typical public liability policy with particular reference to these principles of contract law. However, it has to be realised that it is increasingly the practice to provide liability cover as part of a package, eg traders' combined or contractors' indemnity policy, and that there is no such document as a *standard* public liability policy. Nevertheless, the fundamental content of the liability cover within such "package" policies follows a similar structure and direct reference will therefore be made to the policy in Appendix A. Policies issued by Sun Alliance Insurance Group and Colonia Insurance (UK) Limited are also reproduced as examples of the type of policy currently available.

The public liability policy differs from contracts of property insurance in that, subject to policy limits where applicable, the amount to be paid by insurers is not primarily determined by the terms and conditions of the policy, but by the extent to which the policyholder is liable at law to compensate the party suffering loss, injury or damage.

Subject to specific conditions and circumstances the policy therefore provides an indemnity in respect of the insured's legal liability to pay compensation and damages to third parties, ie persons not party to the contract. If there is a legal liability, then the amount to be paid will usually be determined by negotiation or, if agreement cannot be reached, by the courts.

A legal liability can be incurred in a number of ways which fall into three principal categories:

(a) the common law as developed by the courts over many years;
(b) under contract as agreed between the parties;
(c) statutory liability as laid down by Parliament.

It is not the intention of liability insurance to offer an indemnity in respect of all types of liability as policies are generally restricted to provide cover in respect of events which are accidental from the point of view of the insured and which result in bodily injury or physical damage. There would not, therefore, be any indemnity provided for damages awarded in respect of libel, slander or false imprisonment (although insurance cover is available for these liabilities) as in most cases this would result from a deliberate act and not give rise to physical injury.

One party to a contract may agree to pay compensation to the other if he or she does not complete the contract within a specified time. This is a liability which only arises because of the particular terms of the agreement and would not be incurred at common law. Such contractual liabilities are specifically excluded from the cover afforded by most policies.

Damages may be awarded against the policyholder, and an indemnity is provided by the liability policy, for liabilities incurred under the following areas of the law.

Negligence

Negligence is a tort (a civil wrong as opposed to a criminal wrong) which has developed under the common law. It has been defined as the omission to do something which a reasonable person, guided by those considerations which ordinarily regulate the conduct of human affairs, would do, or doing something which a prudent and reasonable person would not do (*Blyth v Birmingham Waterworks Co* (1856)).

In order to succeed in an action for negligence the plaintiff (the party that has suffered the wrong) must prove three things:

(a) that the defendant owed him or her a duty of care;
(b) that there has been a breach of that duty; and
(c) that he or she has sustained injury or damage as a result of that breach.

The onus of proof generally rests on the plaintiff (claimant) and in the civil courts is based on the "balance of probabilities", rather than "proof beyond reasonable doubt" as is the case in criminal actions.

Nuisance

This is also a tort and has been defined as the wrong done to a person by unlawfully disturbing him or her in the enjoyment of his or her property or, in some cases, in the exercise of a common right (*Law of Tort*, third edition, Winfield).

Nuisance is a difficult area of the law and although it is generally thought that liability can arise even though all reasonable care has been taken and is thus distinguishable from negligence, there is authority for suggesting that some element of fault must be present, as in the following example.

Encroachment of tree roots into neighbouring property gives rise to liability in nuisance and was once thought to be a strict liability, ie once damage was proved by the plaintiff a liability automatically arose irrespective of fault on the part of the person responsible for the tree. However, recent case law (*Greenwood v Portwood* [1985]) suggests that the owner of the tree or occupier of the land on which it grows is only liable if he or she knew, or ought to have known, that the roots could cause damage to his or her neighbour's property. Escape of dust, fumes, smells and noise are other examples of nuisance.

In the case of a continuing nuisance the courts will grant the plaintiff an injunction preventing the defendant from carrying on the activity which causes the nuisance. If this activity does not give rise to any physical harm to the plaintiff or to his or her property there is no indemnity under the policy even though the defendant may suffer financial loss by complying with the injunction.

If, for example, a contractor was constructing a new road and the work gave rise to a great deal of noise and dust, legal actions may be brought by local residents to stop construction work at night and by farmers for dust damage to crops. The court might grant an injunction to the local residents preventing the contractors from working at night and also award the farmer damages for loss of his or her crop. The public liability policy would indemnify the contractor in respect of the damages awarded to the farmer but give no indemnity for the inevitable financial loss to the contractor as a result of being prevented from working at night in order to finish the contract on time and thus possibly avoid penalty payments to the employer.

Trespass

Trespass is another tort, but one which can give rise to a criminal action. It is an unlawful act committed with force and violence on the person or property of another. Although some degree of violence is necessary, the slightest degree is sufficient. It may be thought that a liability for trespass could not fall within the term of a liability policy as it involves an act of a deliberate nature. Consider, however, the following circumstances. A firm involved in carrying out geological surveys obtains permission to enter onto a farmer's land for the purpose of laying a line of explosive charges in the ground. Because of a setting-out error some charges are laid in a field for which access has not been granted and when the charges are set off damage is caused to the drainage system in that field. There is no doubt that the survey company would be liable for trespass but would the policy indemnify them? In these circumstances the answer must be "yes" because, although the act of exploding the charges was deliberate, the consequences, ie damage to the drainage system, were wholly accidental from the point of view of the insured firm.

Strict liability

The law imposes certain liabilities even where the defendant has exercised all reasonable care. Such a liability arises under what is referred to as the rule in *Rylands v Fletcher* (1868), a case involving the escape of water from the defendant's reservoir into the plaintiff's mine. The defendant was held liable on the grounds that the occupier of land who brings and keeps upon it anything likely to do damage if it escapes is bound at his or her peril to prevent its escape, and is liable for all the direct consequences of its escape even if he or she has been guilty of no negligence. In addition, however, for the "rule" to apply it must be shown that the defendant was making "non-natural" use of the land. This is a difficult concept to understand and is open to various interpretations. In one sense it could mean that the land is being used in such a way as to bring with it an increased danger to others. An alternative interpretation is that the dangerous thing is not normally present on the land in the ordinary course of nature, such as something which grows naturally or a natural accumulation of rainwater. It is suggested that the second approach is probably what was intended as otherwise there would be very little difference between *Rylands* and negligence.

Strict liability is often confused with *absolute* liability but they differ in that defences are available to an action involving strict liability, for example, default of the claimant or Act of God, but there is no defence in the case of absolute liability.

The law very rarely imposes an absolute liability. For example, it is sometimes suggested that the Water Act 1984 imposes an absolute liability on water authorities for damage caused by burst water mains owned by an authority or under its control, but the defences of contributory negligence and that the escape of water was caused by the person suffering the loss are available.

Despite criticism of insurers in the media and a widely held misconception that they will endeavour to avoid settling claims, it should be noted that the vast majority of liability claims are dealt with by negotiation without the courts ever becoming involved.

In 1978 a report was issued by The Royal Commission on Civil Liabilities under the chairmanship of Lord Pearson (the Pearson Report). This recommended certain changes to the method of compensation for personal injuries and, in particular, limited forms of strict liability.

The British Insurance Association carried out a survey for the Pearson Commission which showed that 86 per cent of claims are settled without the issue of a writ and only one per cent of claims reach the courts. The survey also revealed that nearly half of all claims on insurers (those in which they are indemnifying the legal liability of policyholders) are dealt with within 12 months of the injury, and that some payment is made in 97 per cent of these claims. The average period from the date of claim to the date of disposal was nine and a half months, but in some cases could be as much as five years. The Pearson Committee commented that much of the delay is inherent in a legal system which is adversarial in nature and often reliant on agreed medical reports.

There is also a good deal of confusion due to the use of the word "claim" and the fact that it is used in different contexts or to mean different things in the same context. *Chambers Twentieth Century Dictionary* defines "claim" as, ". . . a demand for something supposed due: right or ground for demanding . . .". Several different claims or demands can arise out of one incident. For example, suppose the owner of a house (Mrs Jones) discovers that her property has been damaged because of tree roots spreading from a neighbour's (Mr Smith) garden. The following claims are possible.

(a) Mrs Jones may make a claim against her insurers, ie the policy covering the buildings which are damaged.
(b) Mrs Jones may not have insurance cover and thus would have to make a claim against her neighbour.
(c) If she does have cover her insurers would look to recover or claim their outlay from Mr Smith.
(d) Mr Smith could claim on a policy providing an indemnity in respect of his legal liabilities.

It is probably fair to say that most people would think that these were all "insurance claims" and that therefore any problems in settling the claim were the fault of the insurers. There are in fact several ways in which this matter could be resolved but, assuming that Mrs Jones has no insurance cover for this event, she will have to show that Mr Smith is legally liable if she is to obtain compensation for the damage caused. This legal "claim" could well lead to a protracted dispute or ultimately, legal proceedings, if Mr Smith or his insurers consider that he is not legally liable. This is not an "insurance" dispute because it could well arise even if Mr Smith had no insurance. The insurance company is involved because they have issued a policy which indemnifies Mr Smith in respect of his legal liabilities. They would therefore deal with his claim under the policy because they are contractually bound to do so, but would not settle the claim from Mrs Jones for the damaged property if there was no legal liability for that damage. It is therefore important to differentiate between a claim between two parties where one is seeking to recover damages from the other because of loss, damage or injury caused as a result of the breach of some legal duty owed by the latter to the former, and a contractual claim under an insurance policy whether in respect of damage to property covered or in respect of an indemnity provided.

It is worth reiterating, however, that a public liability policy is intended to indemnify the insured for legal liability to third parties arising in specified circumstances. It does not cover all the insured's legal or moral responsibilities to third parties.

Having discussed, albeit briefly, the objective of the policy it is now necessary to consider the structure of the policy by examining each of the parts into which it is divided.

Although content may differ considerably most policies follow a similar pattern and are made up of the following sections.

Recital clause

This section defines the parties (generally two, but there may be more if the insurance is in joint names) to the contract of insurance and makes reference to the consideration received in the form of a premium.

Operative clause

This sets out the circumstances in which one party to the contract (the insurer) will indemnify the other(s) (the insured) in the event of certain defined circumstances arising.

In addition to meeting any claim for damages for which the insured might be liable, the insurer will usually agree to meet legal costs.

Proviso clause

This clause defines the limits of indemnity provided by the insurer during the policy period.

Policy exceptions

As the operative clause is fairly brief and worded in such a way as, on its own, would provide the insured with cover far wider than intended by the insurer, it is necessary for the policy to include a substantial number of exceptions. It is therefore important to realise that the indemnity provided is defined as much by these exceptions or exclusions as by the operative clause.

Policy conditions

All contracts are subject to certain conditions, whether implied or specified and a contract of insurance is no exception. The conditions are the terms governing the agreement between insurer and insured. In addition to the conditions set out in the policy document other, equally important, conditions are implied such as the duty of utmost good faith common to all policies of insurance which requires the insured to disclose all material facts to the insurer.

Endorsements

Endorsements are special clauses which vary the standard policy cover. Standard in this context means the basic cover provided by a particular insurer. It is now common for the endorsements to be numbered and printed within a standard format as part of the basic document, and then to incorporate the specific endorsement(s) into the policy as required by reference to the relevant number(s) in the policy schedule. This allows the insurer to print one standard document and then tailor it to individual requirements.

Policy schedule

The schedule contains all the variable information such as the name and address of the insured, limits of indemnity and, as mentioned above, the numbers of any operative endorsements. The information on the schedule is usually typed or written and is often in the form of a separate piece of paper to be inserted into the policy document.

CHAPTER 2

The recital clause

Whereas the Insured carrying on the Business described in the Schedule and no other for the purposes of this insurance by a proposal and declaration which shall be the basis of this contract and be deemed to be incorporated herein has applied to the Company for the insurance hereinafter contained and has paid or agreed to pay the Premium as consideration for or on account of such insurance.

The "insured"; the "company"

The recital clause identifies the insured and the company as the parties to the contract.

The words "insured" and "company" are defined in the policy. The insured is identified by name and address in the policy schedule. The term "insured" can be extended, usually by endorsement, to include others such as agents or sub-contractors of the named insured. It is the person(s) identified in the policy as the insured who will be able to receive an indemnity under the policy.

It is most important that the business of the insured is accurately described when the proposal for insurance is completed. The insurer will assess the risk on the basis of the nature of the business and the premium is usually calculated by applying a certain rate per cent to either the turnover or the wage-roll of the insured. The insurer's claims statistics will show which types of business are more likely to give rise to claims and they are rated accordingly.

It is fairly obvious, for example, that a demolition contractor will attract a higher rate than a builder engaged in the construction of private houses. Whilst it may be thought that it is a straightforward matter for a correct business description to be given, problems frequently arise, particularly when companies expand their business operations. For example, the owner of a small garden centre on a busy main road may decide to open a café on the premises. Some years ago that may have seemed an innovative idea but today it is by no means unusual to find some form of eating facilities at a garden centre. Is this something which the owner should tell the insurers about and, if they are not informed what will happen if a claim has to be made as a result of a customer being injured when hot food is dropped by a member of staff in the café?

Firstly, it is necessary to consider whether the expansion of the business to include a café is a material change in risk. In effect this means, is it a factor which would affect the rating of the risk and thus the premium to be charged?

S. 18(2) of the Marine Insurance Act 1906 states:

> Every circumstance is material which would influence the judgment of a prudent insurer in fixing the premium or determining whether he will take the risk.

Unfortunately this does not resolve the problem; surely it is unreasonable to expect the proposer to know all the factors that affect the judgement of an experienced underwriter. Certainly, even a person with no underwriting skill would realise that a demolition contractor, for example, would be a greater risk than a shopkeeper but would the garden centre owner expanding into catering appreciate that this side of the business could be rated differently?

Utmost good faith

The law does not generally require that one party to a transaction should reveal information to the other party of which the other is not aware. In certain circumstances it would clearly be inequitable to allow this situation and thus, where one party has a considerable knowledge of facts which are material to the subject matter of the contract, whereas the other is ignorant of these facts, the principle of *utmost good faith* applies. The party with knowledge of these facts must disclose them even if he or she is not asked about them. Insurance contracts come within this category and, following the principle of utmost good faith, both the insured *and the insurer* are under a duty to disclose all material facts.

Duty of disclosure

As explained by Lord Mansfield in the case of *Carter v Boehm* (1766) the duty of disclosure is imposed on those seeking insurance because:

> Insurance is a contract upon speculation. The special facts upon which the contingent chance is to be computed lie most commonly in the knowledge of the assured only; the underwriter trusts to his representation, and proceeds upon confidence that he does not keep back any circumstances in his knowledge to mislead the underwriter into a belief that the circumstance does not exist. The keeping back of such a circumstance is a fraud and therefore the policy is void. Although the suppression should happen through mistake, without any fraudulent intention, yet still the underwriter is deceived and the policy is void; because the risk run is really different from the risk understood and intended to be run at the time of the agreement. . . . Good faith forbids either party, by concealing what he privately knows, to draw the other into a bargain from his ignorance of the facts and his believing to the contrary.

The proposition that the duty of utmost good faith is imposed not only on the insured but also on the insurer was stated in *Carter v Boehm* (1766) and recently affirmed by the Court of Appeal in *Banque Financière De La Cité SA v Westgate Insurance Company Limited* in which the minimum duty owed by an insurer to the insured was stated as:

> . . . the duty falling on the insurer must at least extend to disclosing all facts known to him which are material either to the nature of the risk sought to be covered or the recoverability of a claim under the policy which a prudent insured would take into account when deciding whether or not to place the risk for which he seeks cover with that insurer.

It is difficult to know the extent of the insurer's duty in respect of the *nature of the risk* as, in nearly all circumstances, this is a matter about which the insured will have most knowledge, but it seems possible that difficulties could arise for insurers in relation to their duty regarding *recoverability of a claim*.

Insurers frequently grant cover before the policy is issued, either by means of a cover note or a letter, stating that cover is in force "subject to the company's normal terms and conditions". If, when the policy is issued, the insured discovers that it includes onerous conditions or exceptions which have a bearing on the very reason for which cover was obtained, and which had not previously been revealed by the insurer, it seems that the insured would be entitled to avoid the policy and obtain the return of the premium paid.

The duty to disclose material facts does not only arise when the insurance is sought but, as liability policies are normally issued for a period of one year, there is a new contract at renewal and the insured is again under a duty to disclose material facts (*Stokell v Heywood* [1897]).

There have been attempts to reduce the onerous duty on the insured by defining the test of materiality as the duty to disclose such facts as the particular insured believes to be material or the duty to disclose such facts as a reasonable man would believe to be material.

In 1954 the Law Reform Committee were asked to consider special conditions and exceptions in insurance policies and the effect of non-disclosure on the liability of insurers.

The report was issued in 1957 and, in dealing with this subject, stated:

> The effect of non-disclosure may be considered first since it is a consequence of the general law relating to insurance contracts and does not involve any express term or condition. We take it to be well settled law,
> (a) that the duty of disclosure of material facts – or the rule of uberrima fides as it is often called – applies to all classes of insurance and,
> (b) that the question in every case is whether the fact not disclosed is material to the risk and not whether the insured, whether reasonably or otherwise, believed or understood it to be so. Further, we see no reason to doubt that the definition of "material" adopted by the Privy Council in Mutual Life Insurance Company of New York v Ontario Metal Products Company Limited for the purposes of life insurance – namely that the fact, if disclosed, might have led a reasonable insurer to decline the risk or to stipulate a higher premium – would be applied in all classes of insurance. This definition is substantially the same as that laid down in the Marine Insurance Act 1906, and has been adopted by an English court as a definition of materiality for the purposes of subsections 3 and 5 of s. 10 of the Road Traffic Act 1934 (Zurich General Accident and Liability Insurance Company v Morrison).
>
> The practical effect of the law on this point is that insurers are entitled to repudiate liability wherever they can show that a fact within the knowledge of the insured was not disclosed which, according to current insurance practice, would have affected their judgement of the risk. Whether the insuring public at large is aware of this it is difficult to say; but it seems to us to follow from the accepted definition of materiality that a fact may be material to insurers, in the light of the great volume of experience of claims available to them, which would not necessarily appear to a proposer for insurance, however honest and careful, to be one which he ought to disclose.

The Law Reform Committee recommended a change in law such that, for the purpose of any contract of insurance, no fact shall be deemed material unless it would have been deemed material by a reasonable insured. Nevertheless, the law has not been changed and in *Lambert v Co-operative Insurance Society Ltd*, a case heard in the Court of Appeal in 1975, the insured, Mrs Lambert, failed in her case against insurers who had declined to meet her claim for the theft of her jewellery because she had not disclosed the fact of her husband's recent conviction when she was renewing the policy. It is interesting to note, however, that all three Lords of Appeal in that case considered that the law as it stood was unjust and that the recommendation of the Law Reform Committee should be implemented.

Other cases where the insured has failed to recover under the policy include *Roselodge v Castle* (1966), where the insured company claimed after a diamond robbery but had not disclosed the previous conviction of its sales manager for smuggling diamonds, *Horne v Poland & Others* (1922) where it was held to be a material fact that the insured was an alien from an eastern country who had assumed an English name; and *Woolcott v Sun Alliance and London Assurance* (1978), where the court accepted that failure of the insured to disclose a criminal conviction was material as that conviction increased the "moral hazard" so that the insurance company would not have accepted the risk had it known about the conviction.

On the other hand in *Reynolds and Anderson v Phoenix Assurance Co Ltd* (1978) a minor conviction for theft many years previously was held not to be material.

Most liability insurers require a signed proposal form and it could be argued therefore that, in presenting such a form to proposers, insurers have ample opportunity to ask questions about matters which they would consider to be material for that particular risk. They are also protected by policy conditions, warranties and endorsements restricting their exposure against any particularly hazardous risks not allowed for in the premium rating.

In general most proposal forms do bring out sufficient information to enable the prospective insurer to understand the business and associated risks and, in the event that the proposer's business involves special hazards, a prudent underwriter would ask further questions before calculating a premium and deciding on what terms the policy should be issued. (A typical proposal form is shown in Appendix B.) Obtaining such information can be a fairly prolonged affair involving correspondence and meetings between proposer, possibly a broker and the underwriter, and producing a substantial "underwriting file". The information given by the proposer (and the broker on his behalf) forms part of the contract and is subject to the usual declaration on the proposal form, plus, of course, the principle of utmost good faith. Nevertheless, the answers given on the proposal or in subsequent correspondence prior to issue of the policy only reveal the state of affairs which existed at that time and the policyholder is then under a duty to disclose other material facts at renewal (*Hair v Prudential Assurance Co Ltd* [1984]).

Despite the comments in judgements given in the *Lambert* case insurance contracts were excluded from the provisions of the Unfair Contract Terms Act (1977) and the Association of British Insurers agreed to issue a Statement of Insurance Practice (see Appendix E). It should be noted that this applies to general insurances of policyholders resident in the United Kingdom and insured in their private capacity only. It does not, therefore, apply to any form of commercial enterprise. Nevertheless, in practice insurers do not make unreasonable use of their rights to avoid a policy in the event of non disclosure or innocent misrepresentation.

Breach of duty/warranty

If the proposal form is answered truthfully according to the proposer's knowledge and belief then it is most unlikely that the insurer will seek to avoid the policy for non-disclosure or innocent misrepresentation. However, it should be fully appreciated that a breach of the duty to disclose and/or the breach of warranty in the proposal declaration does, as the law stands at the moment, allow the insurer to repudiate liability under the contract, whether the breach is directly relevant to the circumstances leading to the claim or not (*Mackay v London General Insurance* [1935]). Answers to questions in the proposal form are converted into conditions of the policy by the declaration on the proposal form (see Appendix B) that the answers shall be the basis of the contract.

Continuing duty

The question arises to see whether the insured is under a continuing duty to disclose material facts after the policy has been issued, ie the contract is in force.

Most public liability policies are issued for a period of one year and although the insured is under a duty to disclose material facts at renewal the insurer would not be able to avoid the policy for breach of the insured's duty of utmost good faith if there was a material change in risk during the intervening 12 months. In *Woolfall and Rimmer Ltd v Moyle* (1942) a proposal form for employers' liability asked the question: "Are your machinery, plant and ways properly fenced and guarded and otherwise in good order and condition?" The answer given was "Yes" and it was contended by insurers that the question was not limited to the date of the proposal form but continued during the currency of the policy. It was held by the Court of Appeal that there was no justification whatsoever in reading into the question any element of a continuing state of affairs and that it was merely to enable insurers to find out the character of the risk. It should be noted however that the Recital Clause in the specimen policy states: "carrying on the Business described . . . and no other for the purposes . . .". The insurer would therefore, because of the wording of the policy, be entitled to refuse an indemnity in the event of a claim arising out of a change in the business and, in the case of the garden centre proprietor, it would certainly be necessary to notify the insurers of the change in the business before renewal of the policy, in order to have cover for the catering activities.

Waiver of right to repudiate

Having said this, the decision in a case which came before the Court of Appeal in May 1989 suggests that in certain cases, by presenting a proposal form, insurers may waive any right which they might have had to repudiate on the basis that the insured had failed to disclose a material fact (*Roberts v Plaisted (1989) 2 Lloyd's Rep 341*). Interestingly this case concerns an issue which is comparable to the example of the garden centre proprietor and the café, namely the proprietor of an hotel who ran a discothèque on the hotel premises.

In March 1984 Mr Kenneth Roberts, the owner of the Crossroads Motel in Anglesey, arranged insurance cover for the motel through a broker, Mr Allen Brown. The proposal form, which was for hotels, restaurants, clubs and other catering establishments, was completed by Mr Brown and, in response to a question asking whether the premises were occupied for any purposes other that an hotel or a list of activities (which did not include discothèque) given on the proposal, the answer "No" was given. A policy was issued and on 10.2.86 a fire occurred and Mr Roberts claimed in respect of damage to the buildings. Insurers repudiated the claim on the grounds that, *inter alia*, the insured had failed to disclose the fact that a discothèque was being operated at the premises and that this amounted to non-disclosure of a material fact.

The judge in the High Court found in favour of Mr Roberts, and Mr

P S Plaisted, the nominated representative underwriter, appealed against this decision.

Having heard expert evidence, presumably from experienced underwriters, the Court of Appeal accepted that the activity of running a discothèque was a material fact. However their Lordships held that:

(a) if the discothèque was part and parcel of the whole motel operations carried on at the premises, there was no need to disclose it in answer to the question asking if the premises were occupied for purposes other than as an hotel or a list of activities given on the form;
(b) at the date of the proposal it was generally accepted that hotels catering for customers other than residents could well provide a discothèque for non-residents;
(c) if the operation of the discothèque was considered to be material at the time when the proposal form was prepared it did not rate as an exceptional risk so as to be included in a supplementary question, as did the operation of a casino; once this position was established it was clearly waived by the questions in that form;
(d) the judge was justified in coming to the conclusion that, by presenting the proposal form, the insurers waived any right which they might have had to repudiate on the basis that the insured had failed to disclose that he was operating a discothèque at the motel.

The decision in this case has not altered the common law position whereby there is a duty on the proposed insured to disclose all facts material to an insurer's appraisal of the risks which are known or deemed to be known to the insured, but not known or deemed to be known to the insurer. The decision is based on the fact that, in the particular circumstances under consideration and the nature of the questions asked by the insurer on the proposal form, the insurers waived any right which they may have had to repudiate on the grounds of non-disclosure. It should also be noted that in *Carter v Boehm*, previously referred to, the judgement refers to the fact that some matters were deemed to be within public knowledge and thus need not be disclosed. In other words the underwriter should have known about them amd it is not unreasonable to suggest that he should have known that a hotel would run a discothèque, especially in the context of a special hotel insurance scheme.

Agency

A further notable aspect of this case is that information about the discothèque appears to have been given to Mr Brown, a Lloyd's broker, but not disclosed by him to insurers. Commenting on this in his judgement Lord Justice Purchas stated:

> To the person unacquainted with the insurance industry it may seem a remarkable state of the law that someone who describes himself as a Lloyd's broker who is remunerated by the insurance industry and who presents proposal forms and suggested policies on their behalf should not be the safe recipient of full disclosure; but that is the position as it stands at the moment. . . . Perhaps it is a matter which might attract the attention at an appropriate moment of the Law Commission.

This statement refers to the question of agency, a consideration of which is outside the scope of this book, but it should be noted that when an insurance broker completes a proposal on behalf of a client, the proposer, the broker is acting as agent for the client even though he or she may also have some form of agency (remuneration) agreement with the insurer. The proposer must sign the form himself or herself and it is therefore very important that all the answers should be checked carefully. In the case quoted above it is possible that the broker could have been faced with an action for professional negligence had Mr Roberts failed to recover from insurers, on the grounds that he (the broker) was aware of the discothèque, and with his professional knowledge, should have revealed this to the underwriter.

CHAPTER 3

The operative clause

Now this policy witnesseth that the Company will subject to the terms exceptions limits and conditions contained herein or endorsed hereon indemnify the insured against all sums which the insured shall become legally liable to pay as damages in respect of:
1. Accidental bodily injury to any person;
2. Accidental loss of or damage to property;
happening in connection with the Business and occurring within the Territorial Limits during the Period of Insurance.

This is the most important clause of the policy as it defines the circumstances in which insurers will provide an indemnity in accordance with the contract they have entered into with the insured.

The contract

It states that the policy document is evidence of that contract. This is an important point because it must be remembered that the contract itself incorporates the proposal and any other documents or information passing between the parties which formed the basis of the insurer's offer to insure on terms and at a premium accepted by the insured.

There are many variations on the wording used which can bring about fundamental variations to the cover provided. Even what appear to be very minor changes can result in substantial alterations to the level of indemnity provided.

Consider, therefore, the interpretation of this clause if the words ". . . legally liable to pay as damages *in respect of:* – ", were replaced by, ". . . legally liable to pay as damages *in consequence of* . . .". an interpretation of the first wording could be that the insurer will provide the indemnity for the insured's liability to pay damages awarded for, or relating to, (in respect of) injury to the person or for loss or damage to property but not for the consequential financial loss which might arise from the injury or damage, even though the insured has a liability for that financial loss.

Whilst it should be said that it is highly unlikely that any insurer would place such an interpretation on that wording it does give rise to uncertainty which is overcome by the change to the "as a consequence of" wording.

The policy is of course subject to the terms, exceptions, limits and conditions all of which will affect the extent to which the insured will be able to obtain an indemnity in the event of a claim being made against him or her. Each of these will be dealt with in later chapters.

Liability to pay

In agreeing to provide an indemnity for all sums which the insured shall become legally liable to pay the insurer is in effect saying, "if the court finds that you are liable and awards damages we will pay those damages". Therefore, strictly speaking, the liability to pay damages does not arise until the court has determined that there is a liability and the amount of money to be paid as damages is established. In practice, however, the insurer takes over the conduct of the claim immediately it is notified and, in the majority of cases, the matter is resolved without the involvement of any litigation.

Nevertheless, despite this being accepted practice and obviously the most sensible way to proceed in order to prevent excessive costs, as well as being of benefit to the legal process as a whole by reducing the workload of the courts, the decision in *Post Office v Norwich Union Fire Insurance Society Ltd* (1967) confirmed that the insurer is under no obligation to make any payment unless liability has been established by the courts. The case concerned The Third Parties (Rights Against Insurers) Act 1930 a statute intended to be of benefit to third parties in circumstances where the insured party against whom they are claiming becomes insolvent. Prior to the Act any money recoverable under a policy covering the liability of the insolvent insured would have been added to the assets of the insured and the third party would have had no better claim than the general creditors. The Act remedied this situation by tranferring to the third party the rights of the insured to indemnity under the policy so that the insurers are under the same liability to the third party as they were to the insured. In most circumstances the amount of the liability of the insurer to the insured differs from the amount of the liability of the

The operative clause

insured to the third party. This is dealt with by s. 1, subsection 4 of the Act, which states:

> . . . (a) if the liability of the insurer to the insured exceeds the liability of the insured to the third party, nothing in this Act shall affect the rights of the insured against the insurer in respect of the excess; and
> (b) if the liability of the insurer to the insured is less than the liability of the insured to the third party, nothing in this Act shall affect the rights of the third party against the insured in respect of the balance.

The Act also provides that the rights of the third party are not affected by any agreement or settlement reached between the insured and insurer after the liability to the third party has been incurred and that any policy condition attempting to avoid the provisions of the Act is void.

In the *Post Office v Norwich Union* case the Post Office was the third party and was claiming in respect of damage to an underground communication cable caused by contractors insured with Norwich Union. The contractors denied liability on the grounds that they had been given incorrect information about the position of the cable by a Post Office employee. Before legal proceedings were started the contractors went into liquidation and the Post Office sued Norwich Union claiming that it was entitled to the benefit of the policy under the Third Parties (Rights Against Insurers) Act 1930. It was held that the Post Office had no claim on the policy until judgement had been obtained against the contractors. This was because the right to indemnity under the policy did not arise until the insured's liability to pay the third party had been ascertained and the Post Office had no better rights to the policy under the Act than the insured.

The Third Parties (Rights Against Insurers) Act 1930 was also under consideration in *M/S Aswan Engineering Establishment Company v Iron Trades Mutual Insurance Company Limited* (1988) but this case is of particular interest as the judge gave guidance on the meaning of the words "liable at law", a phrase used in the operative clause of some policies.

The plaintiff, Aswan, suffered loss due to a breach of contract by its supplier, which was insured with the defendant, Iron Trades. As the supplier had become insolvent Aswan commenced an action against Iron Trades under the Third Parties (Rights Against Insurers) Act. The operative clause of the policy which Iron Trades had issued to the supplier was in the following terms:

> . . . against all sums which the Insured shall become liable at law to pay as damages and such sums for which liability in tort or under statute shall attach to some party or parties other than the insured but for which liability is assumed

by the Insured under indemnity clauses incorporated in contracts or agreements.

Iron Trades argued that the wording of the policy excluded contractual liability but Mr Justice Hobhouse gave judgement for Aswan. He said that the meaning of "liability at law" was to be determined by reference to the ordinary use of language and that it should not be given any restricted interpretation to accord with the insurer's intentions if the words used in its standard form gave rise to any doubt. In the judge's view the meaning of the words was clear and was not restricted to liability in tort.

"Accidental bodily injury and accidental loss of or damage to property"

This phrase would, at first sight, appear to require very little in the way of explanation. It has already been mentioned that *accidental* means "accidental from the point of view of the insured". In other words, the injury or damage was unintended even if the act that caused it was intentional, as in the example of the survey company causing damage to a farmer's drainage system. If, however, the company had known that the drains were there and still set off the explosive charges, possibly because it would have been too costly or time consuming to remove and resite them, that would not be accidental damage as envisaged by the policy.

The cases of *Filliter v Phippard* (1847) and *Fenton v Thorley* (1903) both considered the word "accidental". In the former it was stated that the word may be employed in contrast to "wilful" and in the latter as "an unlooked for mishap or an untoward event which is not expected or designed".

In recent years some insurers have omitted any reference to "accidental" in the operative clause. Although it is not intended that this development should give increased cover, as non-accidental damage is specifically excluded by a policy exception referring to deliberate act or omission, the effect may well be that the cover provided by such a policy is wider than a policy where the operative clause refers to "accidental damage or injury". This is because it is a principle of law for the insurer to show that an exception or exclusion clause applies to the particular circumstances of a claim, whereas the insured must show that the claim comes within the terms of the operative clause in order to obtain an indemnity.

The words *bodily injury* appear to be specific and unambiguous but is it the intention of insurers to include death, illness, disease and nervous shock or mental distress? Most policies do refer to death, illness and disease and there can be no doubt that it is the intention of insurers to provide an indemnity to the insured for damages awarded in respect of such matters. It is not their intention, however, to indemnify in respect of liability to pay damages for, *inter alia*, wrongful arrest, libel or slander, although the policy can be extended to cover these potential liabilities where necessary.

Nervous shock

In considering the cover afforded in respect of liability to pay damages for nervous shock it is necessary to appreciate that this is an area of the law that has undergone substantial development in the twentieth century, from a point where the courts were very reluctant to recognise nervous shock in the absence of physical injury as a valid head of claim, to a case where damages were awarded to a woman when she visited hospital and learned of the death of one of her children and saw the injuries suffered by the rest of her family as a consequence of a road accident (*McLoughlin v O'Brian and Others* [1982]).

In contrast, in a case heard before the Court of Appeal in 1953 (*King v Phillips*) a mother who heard a boy scream and saw that her son's tricycle had been run over by a taxi was not awarded damages for the shock suffered, on the grounds that the taxi driver owed her no duty of care (see definition of negligence, page 2) as injury to her was not foreseeable.

It seems, therefore, that, as the law stood at that time, there was no need for the policy to refer to nervous shock as no liability could be incurred for nervous shock in the absence of physical injury. This must be contrasted with the situation which has now been reached where the sight of an accident or its aftermath, is actionable, provided of course that the claimant has actually suffered mental harm. It is not, therefore, possible for someone to recover damages merely because they witnessed an accident; there has to be proof of "damage" and the legal principle *injuria sine damno* (no legal remedy in the absence of damage – see explanation of negligence, page 3) still applies although the meaning of "damage" has been expanded.

Even though many policies still refer only to *"bodily* injury" insurers will indemnify in respect of liability incurred to pay damages for nervous shock arising out of an accidental event for which their insured is liable.

Post accident trauma

It is likely that the courts will be called upon to further extend the meaning of "damage" in the legal sense with a potential increase of actions for what is referred to as "post accident trauma". This is a complex condition which has been identified by those who have counselled the victims and witnesses of major tragedies such as the Bradford City Football Club fire and the Zeebrugge disaster. It is known, for example, that police and fire brigade personnel as well as others involved in rescue operations and the families of the victims, have experienced prolonged depression and associated mental problems after such events. How the courts will deal with such claims is not known at the time of writing but it is anticipated that insurers will meet claims on the basis that their policies provide cover in respect of liability for injury and damage and, therefore, if the legal meaning of those words is extended by the courts there can be little doubt that the policies will apply.

Property

The interpretation of *accidental loss of or damage to property* also causes problems, principally related to the definition of "property" and the way in which the law has developed in the area of what is often called "financial loss". It appears to be the intention of insurers that "property" means an article that has a physical existence and some policies seek to clarify any ambiguity by referring to tangible or material property. However, it must be remembered that it is the intention of the policy to indemnify the insured in respect of *legal* liability and it is not unreasonable therefore to consider the legal definition of "property" as opposed to its everyday meaning. According to the *contra proferentem* rule, in the event of ambiguity, the policy will be interpreted in favour of the insured, as the insurers prepared the wording, and the word would be given the widest reasonable meaning in the context of legal liability unless, as is sometimes the case the insurer imposes restrictions by means of policy exceptions.

In English law "property" includes land or chattels and rights relating to them, but also includes rights relating to intangible things, such as a debt. The case of *Hooper v Rogers* (1974) is a good example of a problem that could face an insurer if "property" is not fully defined in the policy. The plaintiff in this case, Hooper, sought an injunction against contractors as he believed that work being carried out by them close to his house threatened to cause damage by removal of support from his premises. The court awarded damages although there was no damage to the plaintiff's premises and the Court of Appeal upheld the award.

In any given situation, therefore, consideration must first be given to whether the insured is legally liable for the damages which are being claimed and then, whether the policy operates, assuming of course that there has been no obvious breach of policy conditions and that no policy exceptions apply.

Economic or financial loss

Problems of policy cover and legal liability frequently occur when a claim is made for economic, or financial, loss in the absence of any obvious "damage" to "property".

Claims for loss of sales due to temporary obstruction of access to premises or for loss of production caused by failure of the power supply due to the insured's negligent actions are common. As an example, consider the following scenario. A civil engineering contractor is employed by the local authority to carry out repairs to the sewerage system in the centre of a busy town. The contract involves deep excavation in the main shopping area which will inevitably cause a certain amount of disruption. During the course of the work an excavator bucket hits and damages a water main. The resulting escape of water causes a major collapse of the road and damage to adjacent underground services.

The following claims are received by the contractor:

(a) From shopkeepers who lose trade because access to their shops is obstructed until the hole in the road is repaired, although they suffer no physical damage.
(b) from a manufacturer on a nearby industrial estate who has lost production because of a break in the electricity supply caused by the incident.
(c) From the electricity board and water authority for damage to their services.

It is assumed that the contractor is negligent, that the contract does not amend its common law liabilities and that the policy in Appendix A applies.

Without dwelling at length on the legal issues involved, it is probable that the contractor would be held liable for the value of lost sales which the shopkeepers could prove arose as a direct result of this incident. But there was no physical damage to the shopkeeper's property, so does the policy apply? The incident was accidental from the point of view of the insured and the policy does not exclude liability resulting from obstruction or denial of access. It could be argued that there has been loss of or damage to property in the legal sense in that the shopkeepers have been deprived of their rights in respect of the business premises which they own and/or occupy, in which case the policy would give an indemnity. It would not cover the trading losses incurred due to the normal progress of the works as this would be the inevitable (and therefore not accidental) result when work of this nature was being carried out. Compensation claims for such losses would possibly be considered by the local authority.

A policy referring to loss or damage to tangible or material property would not provide cover for this claim but some policies, particularly those issued to contractors, do cover accidental obstruction or trespass.

The type of claim referred to in (b) has been the subject of considerable debate in recent years and it is therefore necessary to consider the development of the law relating to financial, or economic, loss which bears some similarity to the previous discussion on nervous shock, as this is a head of damage which arises in the absence of physical harm or damage.

It will be recalled that, for an action in negligence to succeed, the plaintiff must show that the defendant owed a duty of care and that there has been a breach of that duty. For many years the circumstances in which a duty was held to exist were restricted to contractual relationships. For example, the purchaser of a product which caused him or her damage or injury, could succeed in a claim against the seller, but another user of that same product, who was not in contract with the seller, could not.

In the famous case of *Donoghue v Stevenson* (1932) the plaintiff was given a bottle of ginger beer which had been purchased from a retailer by her friend. The bottle contained the decomposed remains of a snail and the plaintiff, having drunk some of the ginger beer, was taken seriously ill. Her claim against the manufacturer succeeded although it was accepted that she had no right in contract against either the retailer or the manufacturer. In his judgement on this case Lord Macmillan stated "the categories of negligence are never closed".

A further major development took place in 1964 when, in the case of *Hedley Byrne and Co Ltd v Heller and Partners Ltd*, it was stated in the House of Lords that there could be liability for a negligent misstatement in a situation where financial loss is suffered without physical damage. Claims in this context would normally come within the indemnity provided by a professional indemnity policy rather than the public liability policy and the policy in Appendix A specifically excludes liability incurred as a result of professional advice.

In this case Lord Devlin suggested that it made no sense to draw any distinction between physical and economic loss but the courts have continued to dismiss claims for pure economic loss arising from negligent acts.

Another well known case involved interruption to the electricity supply caused by negligent excavation by contractors – *Spartan Steel and Alloys Ltd v Martin and Co (Contractors) Ltd (1972)*. As a result of the loss of power molten metal in a furnace solidified and was damaged and production was interrupted.

Spartan claimed for:

(a) loss in value of the metal in the furnace at the time of the interruption of the power supply;
(b) loss of profit on that melt, and;
(c) loss of profit on further melts that could have been produced but for the interruption to the power supply.

It was held that (a) and (b) were recoverable as they resulted from physical damage to the plaintiff's property, but that (c) was not. If the cable which was damaged had belonged to Spartan all heads of claim would have been recoverable; different considerations would have applied if the claim against the contractors had been in contract and not negligence.

A further development in this area of the law occurred with the case of *Junior Books Ltd v The Veitchi Co Ltd* (1982) which had a considerable influence on the insurance market. Veitchi, which was a flooring specialist was employed as nominated sub-contractor (ie it was selected by the employer or its architect) to supply and lay flooring in a factory being built for Junior Books. Not long after completion of the work faults developed in the floor and it became necessary for major repairs to be carried out. Junior Books sued Veitchi for the cost of a replacement floor surface and the financial loss which it would incur because of the disruption of normal operations caused by the remedial work. Veitchi conceded that there was sufficient degree of proximity between it and Junior Books so as to place a duty of care on it in favour of Junior Books in the work of laying the floor. The only issue in dispute was whether that duty extended to the kind of damage being claimed. The defects in the flooring caused no injury or damage to Junior Books' property and there was no contract between Junior Books and Veitchi. This was therefore a claim in negligence for pure economic loss and, guided by previous case law, it is not unreasonable to presume that Junior Books' claim would have failed. However, the House of Lords, by a majority, allowed the claim and stated that there was no reason in logic why pecuniary loss resulting from physical damage should be recoverable whereas pecuniary loss on its own should not (reference Lord Devlin's comments in *Hedley Byrne and Co Ltd v Heller and Partners Ltd* 18 years earlier).

This case caused many insurers to review the cover provided by their liability policies as they assumed that, by using words in the operative clause which referred only to loss of or damage to property there was a serious gap in cover for what was perceived as a "new" legal liability. Unless covered by special endorsement all policies would have excluded the cost of making good the floor itself (see Chapter 6 – Policy Exceptions). *"Financial loss"* cover was therefore offered as an addition to the *standard* cover.

It is questionable whether this was really necessary, particularly bearing in mind the wide legal meaning of the word "property". If insurers are prepared to meet claims for nervous shock without amending policy cover, even where the courts have considerably expanded the type of claim which they are prepared to allow, is there any reason why claims for financial loss should be treated any differently?

Much has subsequently been written about this case and, on reflection, it now seems that the decision did not amount to a fundamental change in the law, principally because it was a case that was decided on its own particular facts, one of which was that the relationship between Junior Books and Veitchi (employer and nominated sub-contractor), although not contractual, was very close to it.

In the recent case of *D & F Estates v Church Commissioners* (1988) it was held that pure economic loss was not recoverable. This was also a case that concerned economic loss resulting from defective work that had to be made good.

From this brief review of the development of the law it will be appreciated that underwriters face considerable difficulties in drafting their policies so that the intended indemnity is granted but at the same time not giving indemnities for legal liabilities which they have no intention of covering.

The operative clause also states that the event must be one that happens in connection with the *business* and occurs within the *territorial limits* during the *period of insurance*. The words in italics are defined in the policy schedule.

The business

The insurer will only provide an indemnity for liabilities incurred by the insured as a result of normal business activities and it is therefore most important that the insurer is informed if there is any change in the nature of the business.

Territorial limits

The policy cover is restricted to events occurring within Great Britain, the Republic of Ireland, Northern Ireland, the Channel Islands and the Isle of Man but there is no restriction for liability incurred in respect of overseas business trips by the insured's employees, unless those employees are engaged in the supervision or execution of any work or contract. In other words the policy will apply to liability incurred outside the territorial limits by employees such as sales representatives and others whilst on overseas trips but not if they or any other employees are engaged on or supervising any type of building or manufacturing project in the country concerned. Most policies now also cover events occurring in member countries of the European Community and on offshore installations in British territorial waters (ie the definition of territorial limits has been extended).

Insurers will make enquiries about the amount and type of overseas work conducted by the insured at the proposal stage and adjust the premium as necessary.

Period of insurance

The event giving rise to the claim against the insured must occur during the period of insurance, which is normally one year from the date of acceptance by the insurer (this is not necessarily the date on which the policy is issued) and for any subsequent annual period for which the insured shall pay and the insurer shall agree to accept a renewal premium, the exact period being defined in the policy schedule. Such a policy is written on what is referred to as a "claims (losses) occurring" basis in contrast to the "claims made" basis. It would in fact be more accurate to refer to "losses" occurring basis, rather than "claims" occurring. As the meaning of these terms is often misunderstood it is hoped that the following illustration will be of assistance to the reader.

In this example the insured, a building contractor has carried out work, part of which was defective and has given rise to a claim for damage or injury.

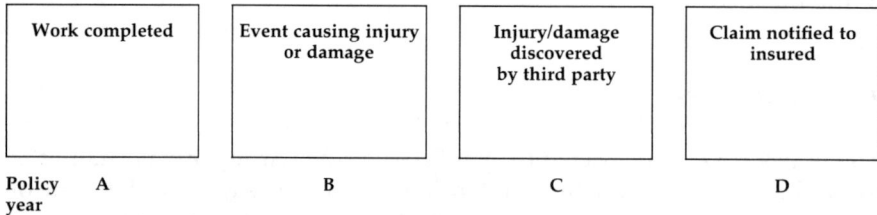

For the purpose of the illustration it is not necessary to consider specific details of the nature of the claim but a fairly typical situation would be where faulty building blocks cause gradual damage to plaster and decorations.

"Losses occurring" policy

Assume firstly that the contractor has a "losses occurring" policy with the same insurer for each period of insurance. The work is completed in policy year A, damage starts to occur in policy year B, but is not discovered by the third party until policy year C, and the claim is notified to the insured in policy year D. Even though the negligent act was during year A and the damage not discovered until year C, this should be dealt with as a claim against the policy in year B because that was when the event causing injury or damage actually occurred. This does not cause a significant problem where there has been a continuity of insurer but disputes between insurers can arise if the insurer has been changed from year to year even if all policies are on a "claims occurring" basis. It may be very difficult, for example, to determine whether the damage first occurred in year B or year C.

"Claims made" policy

If, however, the policy cover over the four year period had been on a "claims made" basis this will be a claim for policy year D. In other words the policy year in which the insured was notified of the claim. This is usually an easily identifiable event and should not give rise to the type of dispute which can arise between "losses occurring" policies for years B and C.

Insurers in the United Kingdom generally issue public liability policies on a "losses occurring" basis.

The alternative "claims made" basis has not generally found favour in the United Kingdom insurance market, but it is the cases where there is a delay betwen "the occurrence" and the manifestation of injury or damage, as in the above example, that led to a move towards the introduction of claims made policies. Such delays occur, for example, in the case of an industrial disease such as asbestosis or industrial deafness. "Claims made" policies are intended to provide cover in respect of claims made against the insured during the policy period irrespective of when the event giving rise to damage or injury actually occurred.

In many cases, however, the claim is made at the time of, or shortly after, the event causing loss, injury or damage, ie the events in policy year B, C and D all take place in year B. In this case both types of policy would cover such a claim, ie the damage or injury happens (occurs) and the claim is made during the policy year B so that the insured would be indemnified whichever form of policy had been issued for that period.

If, however, the insured's negligent act in policy year A causes damage in that year of which the insured has no knowledge, a claim made against a "losses occurring" policy commencing at the start of year B would not indemnify him or her, whereas if it was a "claims made" policy it would.

Problems occur if the insured changes from "claims made" to "losses occurring" at renewal. The claim notified in period D is not covered by a "losses occurring" policy for that period as the damage occurred during a previous period and the "claims made" policies current during periods B and C also fail to indemnify as no claim was "made" during those periods.

It should be noted that the expression "claims made" refers to claims notified to the insured and not to claims against the policy, although this point only becomes significant if the insured is in breach of the policy condition requiring that immediate notification of claims received is given to insurers. However, it is also intended to include circumstances giving rise to loss, injury or damage of which the insured is aware, where there has been no claim but a claim might arise. If the insurer is changed at renewal the insured must inform the new insurer if he or she has any knowledge of such incidents or of claims outstanding.

The problems which can arise are well illustrated by the case of *Thorman and Others v New Hampshire Insurance Company (UK) Ltd and Others* reported in *The Times* on 12.10.87. This case was concerned with a dispute under a professional indemnity policy but the issues involved are of relevance to an understanding of the word "claim" and the problems arising when there is a change of insurer at renewal.

In May 1973 Thorman, a firm of architects, was employed to design a housing development. Problems arose with the brickwork and an action was begun by the building owner by the issue of a writ on 30.6.82, but which was not served on the architects until 20.12.83. Prior to this, between 1976 and 1979, the building owner made a number of complaints which were regarded by the architects as relating to brickwork. Their insurer at the time, New Hampshire, was kept fully informed and was aware that the architects had agreed to share the cost of remedial work. It was not until January 1984, when the statement of claim was served, that it became clear that the building owner's claim extended to other defects in addition to the brickwork. In the meantime, in October 1983, the architects' insurance had been transferred to The Home Insurance Company, the second defendant in this case.

New Hampshire regarded itself as on risk for the defective brickwork alone and told the architects to inform their new insurer of the claim and seek its confirmation that it would indemnify in respect of the other items of the claim. Unfortunately Home did not regard itself as on risk for the additional items, which it submitted were really part and parcel of the the claim which was first notified in July 1979, and therefore a matter for the New Hampshire policy. The dispute came before the Commercial Court in December 1986 when it was decided that The Home Insurance Company was liable to indemnify the architects for the additional defects listed on the statement of claim. However, on appeal to the Court of Appeal this decision was reversed. Sir John Donaldson, Master of the Rolls, stated that a claim within the meaning of the policy is

> . . . the assertion by a third party against the insured of a right to some relief because of a breach by the insured of a duty referred to in section 1 of the policy, and that, if a building owner suffers loss due to faulty workmanship in respect of the floors and roof of the building, and this was notified to the insurer, that might be regarded as one valid claim under the policy.

He had doubts, however, about whether the judge in the Commercial

Court was correct in saying that new and unrelated claims of damage to different parts of the same building would amount to a new claim under the policy. It would, in his Lordship's view, very much depend on the facts.

Sir John Donaldson fully accepted that it was not until this delivery of the statement of claim that the architect realised that matters other than brickwork had gone wrong and were complained of. But what mattered was which claim was being made by the building owner, not which claim was perceived by the insured. In a letter claiming arbitration in June 1982, the building owner had asserted that serious problems had arisen including cracking and damage to brickwork. Apparently it was clear from the correspondence that the claim was in respect of all the serious problems which had arisen by that date and was not confined to the brickwork. The fact that it was unparticularised and uninformative was not relevant – all the matters eventually listed on the statement of claim were in that category and it followed therefore that all were the subject matter of a claim before the New Hampshire came off risk. Furthermore, Lord Donaldson considered that the issue of the writ could be regarded as an occurrence likely to give rise to a claim and that the eventual service of the writ and, at a later date, service of the statement of claim clearly arose out of the issue of the writ.

The appeal by The Home Insurance Company was therefore allowed and it was held that New Hampshire was liable to indemnify the architects in respect of the claims made by the building owner to the exclusion of liability on the part of The Home Insurance Company.

CHAPTER 4

The proviso clause

Provided that the Liability of the Company for all damages payable to any claimant or any number of claimants in respect of or arising out of any one occurrence or in respect of or arising out of all occurrences of a series consequent on or attributable to one source or original cause shall not exceed the Limit of Indemnity specified in the Schedule for any one Period of Insurance.

Limit of indemnity

Having established the circumstances in which insurers will give an indemnity this clause is inserted in order to place a limit on their financial exposure. This is known as the limit of indemnity or limit of liability, and is a sum specified in the schedule.

Although the total amount payable in any one period of insurance is usually unlimited this policy limit applies to any one occurrence, accident, event or series of events consequent on or attributable to one source or original cause. There is usually no financial limit in respect of the value of all claims during the period of insurance. Strictly speaking, therefore, there are two limits of indemnity, one in respect of any one occurrence (as defined in the proviso clause) and the other in respect of any one period of insurance (as defined in the schedule). It is normal, however, for the limit on a product liability policy to be in respect of the period of insurance rather than for any one event claim or occurrence.

The limit of indemnity selected should be for an amount that is adequate for the circumstances of the insured. A private individual may have a limit of £100,000 under the liability section of his or her household policy, whereas a large international corporation could require a limit of £5,000,000 or more.

There is no limit on the amount of damages for which the insured might incur a liability at law other than limits which may be imposed by statute or agreed under contract. Claims arising from a serious fire or explosion caused by the insured's negligence may amount to many millions of pounds and it is therefore necessary for insurers to place some restriction on the amount of indemnity provided by the policy and thus limit their maximum liability. This is not to say that the insured will be unable to obtain insurance to cover his or her maximum potential liability as this can be arranged by means of coinsurance, where different insurers each take an agreed proportion of the risk or by excess of loss insurance where the cover is provided in different "layers". The "primary" insurer would therefore agree to cover all claims up to, say £1,000,000, with excess layer policies operating only when the primary layer has been exhausted.

In the case of coinsurance, one policy is issued by the leading office and other offices take percentages of the risk. The leading office is usually, but not always, the company with the highest proportion, and that company has the authority to handle claims on behalf of all coinsurers. However, where excess of loss insurance is arranged separate policies are issued by the companies responsible for each layer and serious problems can arise if the policies do not have precisely the same wording and definitions of cover.

Should the event giving rise to the claim under the policy result in the insured being liable for damages in excess of the limit of indemnity the insurer can pay to the insured the policy limit and be discharged from any further obligations under the policy (see Condition 3 of the policy in Appendix A). It is not unusual for an insurer to do this if it is apparent at an early stage of enquiries after a claim or incident is notified that the limit of indemnity will be exceeded and that it is liable under the policy to indemnify the insured. By doing this its exposure to the legal costs and expenses of defending the claim, which are payable in addition to the limit of indemnity, is restricted, as otherwise there is no policy limit on the costs which might accrue in defending the claim. They could in fact exceed the Limit of Indemnity.

Any one occurrence

The proviso clause is worded so as to avoid any ambiguity as to what is meant by any one occurrence. Many accidents are uncomplicated and the consequences, in terms of loss, injury or damage, are clearly identified and limited to the time and place of the accident and the persons or property immediately affected.

A large number of claims however are not straightforward as in the following example where a fire which originated in a warehouse had far reaching consequences. A warehouse and its contents were destroyed and damage was caused to neighbouring property as a result of the spread of fire. Toxic chemicals were stored in the building which itself was constructed of materials containing asbestos. Harmful fumes and asbestos dust spread over a wide area and local residents suffered injury after exposure to the fumes. The local authority incurred considerable expense in dealing with the immediate consequences of the problem and in decontaminating the area onto which the asbestos dust has fallen.

For the purpose of this example it is assumed that the fire started as a result of the negligent activities of contractors working for the warehouse owner and that their liability policy was the same as the example in Appendix A, apart from the proviso clause which simply stated: "Provided that the liability of the Company shall not exceed £1,000,000 for any one accident for any one period of insurance". It is also assumed for this illustration that the total damages from all parties will not exceed £1,000,000 and that insurers will not therefore exercise their option to pay the limit of liability.

Problems arise when one has to consider what is meant by "any one accident". The occurrence of the fire causing damage to the building and its contents is clearly one accident but what is the situation with claims from parties remote from the immediate area of the fire who may have suffered injury or damage some considerable time after the fire as a result of exposure to asbestos or hazardous fumes? It could well be argued that these were separate accidents in which case insurers would be liable to pay up to the limit of indemnity for any one claimant, which is not their intention.

The wording of the proviso clause therefore makes it clear that the limit applies to, ". . . any claimant or any number of claimants . . . arising out of any one occurrence . . . or out of all occurrences of a series consequent on or attributable to one source or original cause . . .". This form of words would meet the intention of insurers in the circumstances outlined in the above example, so that the maximum total damages payable to all third parties as a result of this fire would be £1,000,000.

Legal expenses

In respect of a claim for damages to which the indemnity expressed in the policy applies the Company will also indemnify the Insured against:

(a) all costs and expenses of litigation recovered by any claimant from the Insured;

(b) all costs and expenses of litigation incurred with the written consent of the Company:

(c) the solicitor's fee for representation at any coroner's or fatal enquiry or in any court of summary jurisdiction.

The operative clause of the policy states that the insurer will pay damages for which the insured may be legally liable but makes no provision for the payment of other costs and expenses which will almost inevitably be incurred in dealing with any third party claim. Such costs include the expenses incurred in investigating the incident which gave rise to the claim, legal fees of solicitors instructed to deal with any litigation as well as the legal costs incurred by the claimant and recoverable as an award of the court against the insured. As previously stated, these costs are payable in addition to the limit of indemnity. Reference to the operative clause confirms that the indemnity provided is in respect of all sums which the insured shall become legally liable to pay "as damages" and that the proviso clause also refers to the liability of the insurer for "all damages payable" not exceeding the limit of indemnity. There is no mention of costs and expenses although some policies do refer to claimant's costs and expenses in the operative and proviso clauses, in which case they are included within the limit of indemnity, thus reducing the cover to a significant extent where the claim involves prolonged litigation.

The wording of this clause does not place any restriction on the amount payable in respect of costs and expenses but it should be noted that the costs of defending any claim involving litigation are only payable if incurred with the written consent of the insurer. In practice the insurer has probably had a considerable involvement in the handling of such a claim before proceedings are commenced by the claimant and, on becoming aware that a writ is likely to be served on its insured, will have instructed solicitors itself. It is then usual to ask the insured to forward the writ, unacknowledged, either to the insurer or direct to the appointed solicitor, or to nominate the solicitor to accept service. Having instructed the solicitor the insurer will then be responsible for his or her costs and will retain control over the conduct of the litigation. If, however, the insured has a significant financial interest in the matter, either because of a large policy deductible (excess) or because there is some aspect of the litigation for which the policy does not provide an indemnity, agreement may be reached for the costs to be shared on a *pro rata* basis.

Circumstances frequently arise where the commencement of litigation is the first notice that the insured receives of a potential claim under the policy and this can even be where it is the insured who has started the legal action. For example, if a painter and decorator carries out work for which he has not been paid he may instruct his solicitor to commence proceedings to recover that debt (the liability policy does not give cover for the costs of civil litigation of this nature although legal costs and expenses insurance is becoming more readily available). In defence of that action the customer may well say that the bill was not paid because the decorator caused some damage, eg spots of paint on a valuable carpet, and issue a counterclaim for the damage caused. That counterclaim, whether justified or not, is a matter for the liability insurers and they must be notified immediately. When this situation arises most insurers would agree to the solicitors instructed by their insured continuing to deal with the claim on the understanding that the costs of the original action for recovery of the debt be met by the insured and that they (the insurers) have control of the defence of the counterclaim. This would, however, depend on the comparative values of the two parts of the action and the ability and experience of the solicitor concerned.

The third part of this clause provides for payment of solicitor's costs for representation at any coroner's inquest or fatal enquiry or in any court of summary jurisdiction. If an accident occurs which could give rise to a claim under the policy it is in the interest of insurers to have control, on behalf of their insured, over the conduct of the insured's legal representation at any inquest or fatal enquiry touching on the accident, or at any criminal prosecution resulting from the accident. The evidence presented at these hearings will be of considerable relevance to any future civil litigation and it is important that nothing is done which may prejudice the insured's position or the possibility of successfully defending a future claim. It does not follow, however, if the insured is found guilty of a breach of some statutory regulation, that a civil claim against him or her would automatically succeed. It is possible that the regulation was broken innocently and without any fault or blame and, whilst ignorance of the law is no defence to a criminal charge and assuming that the breach does not carry with it an absolute liability for damage or injury caused, a civil claim could be defended on the grounds that there was no negligence on the part of the insured or that the injury or damage was caused as a result of the claimant's own negligence.

Indemnity to personal representatives

In the event of the death of the Insured the Company will in respect of the liability incurred by the Insured indemnify the Insured's personal representatives in the terms of and subject to the limitations of this Policy provided that such personal representatives shall as though they were the Insured observe fulfil and be subject to the terms exceptions and conditions of the policy so far as they can apply.

If the policy is in the name of an individual it does not provide cover for events occurring after the death of the insured but the personal representatives appointed to handle the estate may have to deal with claims in respect of events occurring before the death of the insured. The Law Reform (Miscellaneous Provisions) Act 1934 provides that all causes of action against the deceased survive against his or her estate. This clause therefore protects their position although they are bound by the terms and conditions of the policy in the same way as the named insured.

CHAPTER 5

Exceptions – risks covered by other policies

Insurers seek to restrict the extent of their liability by the introduction of exceptions, which may be classified as follows:
  (a) Exceptions relating to particular causes which, although they may fall within the general indemnities provided by the policy are more specifically covered by a different policy, eg liability risks under motor or employers' liability policies.
  (b) Exceptions relating to causes which are not intended to fall within the scope of the policy but which may possibly do so on account of the general words in which the peril or liability insured against is described, eg contractual liability.
  (c) Exceptions relating to risks which are uninsurable in the normal commercial market, eg war and nuclear risks.

Since exceptions are inserted in the policy mainly for the purpose of exempting insurers from liability for a loss which, but for the exception, would be covered by the policy, they are construed against the insurer with the utmost strictness if there is any ambiguity. It is the duty of insurers to restrict their liability in clear and unambiguous terms and the onus is on the insurers to show that the exception applies in the given circumstances.

The exceptions should, therefore, be read in conjunction with the operative clause and we have already seen in Chapter 3 how these two parts of the policy interact when considering the use of the word "accidental". It will be recalled that some insurers omit this word from the operative clause and seek to exclude "non-accidental" events by an exclusion in the following terms:

> This policy shall not apply to liability in respect of loss injury or damage which results from a deliberate act or omission on the part of the Insured and which

could reasonably have been expected by the Insured having regard to the nature and circumstances of such act or omission.

Clearly this wording has been designed to ensure that the policy will not provide cover for deliberate or wilful acts, bearing in mind the judgments in *Filliter v Phippard* and *Fenton v Thorley* already referred to in Chapter 3.

In addition to consideration of whether the action of the insured was deliberate or wilful the question of "public policy" also enters the equation and this was a matter discussed by the Court of Appeal in *Gray and Another v Barr* (1971). This case arose following the trial and acquittal of Barr for the murder and manslaughter of a friend whom he suspected was having an affair with his wife. During a fight Barr was carrying a loaded shotgun and accidentally shot his friend. The friend's wife sued Barr who sought an indemnity under the liability section of his household policy. The Court of Appeal had to consider whether the death was caused by accident and, by a majority verdict decided that, as a matter of public policy, Barr was not entitled to be indemnified by the policy. Whilst it is perfectly reasonable that a policyholder should not benefit from the results of criminal actions, in the event that he or she has a policy which might provide an indemnity for loss or liability incurred as a direct result of those actions, and to allow such would clearly be undesirable, in this case Barr was acquitted in the criminal courts on the basis that the death was caused by accident.

There seem to be no logical rules as to when the courts will apply the doctrine of public policy; it is more a question of the judiciary saying, "although there are no precedents or rules concerning this matter it would clearly be wrong for the defendant (or plaintiff) to benefit in these circumstances". Nevertheless it is an area of the law which occasionally has a bearing on the interpretation of insurance policies and is therefore of interest in our consideration of the public liability policy.

Exceptions relating to risks covered by other policies

1. Liability in respect of injury to any person under a contract of service or apprenticeship with the Insured where such injury arises out of and in the course of such person's employment or service with the Insured.

This exception is intended to exclude claims in respect of employees as such claims are normally covered under an employer's liability policy, but only refers to injury and would not therefore apply to any claim from an employee for damage to property. It also only applies to injury arising out of and in the course of employment. The wording of this exception should follow the wording of the operative clause of the insured's employer's liability policy to ensure that there is no gap in cover and it is therefore advisable to have both policies with one insurer. This is particularly important in the construction industry where there is a comparatively small "permanent" labour force but a large number of sub-contractors and "labour only" contractors whose legal identity in relation to the insured is frequently the subject of dispute.

In place of the words "under a contract of service" in this exception some policies use the words "in the service of" and the following example demonstrates the sort of problem that can arise if the insured has an employers' liability policy where the operative clause has the former wording and a public liability policy where the exclusion uses the latter wording.

A sub-contractor lends one of his employees to the insured, the main contractor, to carry out work under the direction and control of the insured at a site other than the one at which the two parties have a formal contractual relationship for the duration of a particular building project. It is assumed tht there is no written contract governing this temporary arrangement and that no payment is made for the loan. As a result of the negligence of one of the insured's employees the sub-contractor's employee is injured and the insured looks to his insurers for an indemnity in respect of his vicarious liability for his employee's negligence.

Unfortunately the employers' liability policy will probably not assist as the injured person was not under a contract of service and the public liability policy would also not operate as it excludes injury to any person in the service of the insured, which the loaned employee most certainly was. The main contractor is not therefore protected by either policy.

The two main problems experienced with these exceptions concern the interpretation of "employee" and "course of employment" and it is necessary to consider the legal meaning of these words as well as the associated terms "in the service of" and "contract of service".

The expression "master/servant relationship" is frequently used in cases dealing with this problem in place of "employer/employee" and the normal test applied to decide whether a master/servant relationship exists is to ask who controls what the employee does and how he or she does it. However, this test derives from an 1880 case, *Yewens v Noakes (1880)*, in which it was stated that a person working for another was regarded as a servant if he was "subject to the command of the master as to the manner in which he shall do his work" but that, if the master only directed the servant in "what" was to be done and not "how" it was to be done, the person doing the work was considered to be an independent contractor.

Clearly this test is not adequate for present day circumstances and should only be used as a starting point. In the case of large companies employing highly skilled or professionally qualified staff it is unlikely that the company has control over how those people perform the jobs allotted to them, or that a health authority would tell medical staff how to treat patients. It is even more unrealistic to suggest that a shipping company controls the performance of the captain of a ship or an airline the manner in which a pilot flies an aeroplane. It would not be disputed, however, unless there were special circumstances, that such people were employees and we must therefore consider what test should be applied to the modern day situation.

In *Ready-Mixed Concrete (South-East) Ltd v Minister of Pensions and National Insurance* (1968) MacKenna J, in considering what was meant by a contract of service, stated:

> A contract of service exists if the following three conditions are fulfilled:
>
> (i) The servant agrees that in consideration of a wage or other remuneration he will provide his own work and skill in the performance of some service for his master.
> (ii) He agrees, expressly or impliedly, that in the performance of that service he will be subject to the other's control in a sufficient degree to make that other master.
> (iii) The other provisions of the contract are consistent with its being a contract of service. . . .

There is further assistance in the case *Montreal Locomotive Works Ltd v Montreal and A-G for Canada (1963)* where Lord Wright stated:

> In earlier cases a single test, such as the presence or absence of control, was often relied on to determine whether the case was one of master and servant, mostly in order to decide issues of tortious liability on the part of the master or superior. In the more complex conditions of modern industry, more complicated tests have often to be applied. It has been suggested that a fourfold test would in some cases be more appropriate, a complex involving;
>
> (i) control;
> (ii) ownership of the tools;
> (iii) chance of profit;
> (iv) risk of loss.
>
> Control in itself is not always conclusive. Thus the master of a chartered vessel

is generally the employee of the shipowner though the charterer can direct the employment of the vessel.

Again the law often limits the employer's right to interfere with the employee's conduct, as also do trade union regulations. In many cases the question can only be settled by examining the whole of the various elements which constitute the relationship between the parties. In this way it is in some cases possible to decide the issue by raising as the crucial question whose business is it, or in other words by asking whether the party is carrying on the business, in the case of carrying it on for himself or on his own behalf and not merely for a superior.

Lord Denning in *Bank voor Handel en Scheepvaart NV v Slatford* (1952) put forward the suggestion that the test of being a servant does not rest on submission to orders but depends on whether the person is part and parcel of an organisation.

The Employer's Liability (Defective Equipment) Act 1969 defines employee as "a person who is employed by another person under a contract of service or apprenticeship and is so employed for the purposes of a business carried on by that other person, and 'employer' shall be construed accordingly".

Other factors to be taken into account are the right to hire and fire, the payment of National Insurance contributions, the provision of tools and equipment and how income tax is paid – if PAYE, then there is an inference that the person on whose behalf the tax is paid is an employee.

An employee is said to be engaged under a *contract of service* as against an independent contractor who performs work under a *contract for services*.

The following are examples of contracts for services:

(a) a solicitor engaged to provide advice for a fee;
(b) a plumber carrying out repairs for an agreed payment;
(c) the employment of a landscape gardener who offers his services to the general public to carry out specific work for an agreed charge as against a permanently employed gardener who is paid a regular wage.

Most of the difficulties encountered by insurers concern the position of labour-only sub-contractors in the construction industry. These are usually groups of people under the control of a "labour master" who hire out their labour and arrange for the payment of their own income tax and stamping of National Insurance cards. Apart from the method of payment of wages, tax and National Insurance contributions the relationship between the principal and labour-only sub-contractor differs very little from that of employer and employee in that the principal usually retains the right to hire and fire, controls the work done and the way it is done and frequently provides the necessary tools. It is therefore normal practice for the employer's liability policy to cover his or her legal liabilities to such people and for the public liability policy to include a clause such as:

> Persons under a contract of service or apprenticeship shall include any:
> (i) labour master and persons supplied by him
> (ii) person employed by labour only subcontractors
> (iii) self-employed person
> (iv) person hired from any public authority company firm or individual.
>
> while working for the Insured in connection with the business.

Although it is the intention of the policy to exclude liability in respect of injury to persons who, bearing in mind the preceding discussion, may generally be called employees, it does of course cover the insured's vicarious liability for the acts of such persons. Having attempted to establish when an employer/employee relationship exists it is then necessary to consider what is meant by "in the course of employment" as this is again an area which has been the subject of much litigation.

Two examples of the sort of situation which can arise will be considered.

(a) A petrol pump attendant believing that a customer had tried to drive away accused the customer, in violent language, of having tried to drive away without paying for the petrol that had been put into the tank of his car. The customer paid the bill, called the police and told the attendant that he would be reported to the employer, whereupon the attendant assaulted and injured the customer.

(b) The owner of a mink stole sent it to a furrier for cleaning who, with her consent, passed it on to another company who knew that it belonged to an unspecified customer of the furrier. Whilst the fur was with this company it was stolen by one of their employees.

Incidents such as these are not unusual and most people would feel that neither of these employees was acting in the course of his employment and that their employers could not be held liable for their actions.

The situation in (a) was considered in *Warren v Henley's Ltd* (1948) where emphasis was placed on whether the act committed by the employee was so connected with the acts which he was expressly or impliedly authorised to do that it was in fact a mode of doing those acts. The judge considered that it was not but that it was an act of purely personal vengeance.

This was contrasted with the case of *Poland v John Parr and Sons* (1926) which came before the Court of Appeal and also concerned an assault committed by an employee. In that case however the employee hit a young boy whom he honestly and reasonably believed was pilfering or about to pilfer goods belonging to the employer.

In his judgement Scrutton LJ stated,

> . . . In order to make a master liable for the act of a person alleged to be his servant, the act must be one of a class of acts which the person was authorised or employed to do. If the act complained of is one of that class, the master is liable, although the act is done negligently, or, in some cases, even if it is done with excessive violence. But the excess may be so great as to take the act in question out of the class of acts which the person is employed or authorised to do.

In (b) the employee was certainly not employed to steal customers' property which had been entrusted to his employer but it was held that the employer was liable as the fur had been given to that particular employee for cleaning and he was therefore acting in the course of his employment. Had the fur been stolen by another employee not employed to do anything in relation to the fur the employer would not have been liable.

Although these cases do not have a direct bearing on the policy exception under consideration as they are concerned with the relationship between the employer and third parties, they do illustrate the difficulty of interpreting the phrase "in the course of employment" which appears in the exclusion.

Of more direct relevance are the cases dealing with the relationship between employer and employee. These usually concern incidents that occur whilst the employee is engaged partly on his or her own and partly on the employer's business and result in disputes as to whether it is an employer's or public liability matter. For example, if an employee having "clocked off" is knocked over and injured at the factory gate by a fellow employee still at work, would the injured employee still be in the course of employment, in which case any claim by him or her would be dealt with by the employer's liability and not the public liability policy?

And what is the situation of employees on meal breaks away from the place of work or travelling between places of work? In *Smith v Stages* (1988) the plaintiff was killed in a car accident which was caused by the negligence of a fellow employee. The two employees were sent from their base in Staffordshire to work in Scotland. Having worked most of the day and all night they set out to drive home immediately and it was on the journey home that the plaintiff was killed. The employer had agreed to pay eight hours' sleeping time and eight hours' travelling time to allow them to return home but did not tell the employees when to travel or what method of transport they should use. It was held by the Court of Appeal that the driver was in the course of employment when the accident occurred as the employer was entitled to direct the employees as to how they should spend the day of the accident and to tell them to take rest breaks, and that therefore the employer was liable.

In contrast, the employer was held not liable in the case *Hilton v Thomas Burton (Rhodes)* (1961) where an employee was also killed in a motor accident caused by the negligent driving of a fellow employee. During working hours the workmen left the place of work in the employer's van to go to a café and the employer gave evidence that he permitted his men to drive the van for any reasonable purpose, which included getting refreshments. It was held, however, that the men were on a frolic of their own and not acting in the course of their employment so that the employer was not liable.

Evidently there is no legal authority to which we can refer for a simple definition or test of when a person is acting in the course of employment to assist in those cases which fall into a "grey" area and each case must be considered individually in the light of the most recent case law.

It is suggested, however, that "in the course of employment" includes not only any act or omission which is actually authorised, expressly or impliedly by the employer, but also an unauthorised, or even a prohibited act, provided that the act is merely a wrongful method of doing an authorised act.

2. *Liability in respect of loss or damage to property:*

   (a) belonging to the Insured.
   (b) in the charge or under the control of the Insured but this exception shall not apply to property belonging to any servant of the Insured.
   (c) caused by or through or in connection with the bursting of any economiser used in conjunction with a steam boiler or any boiler vessel or other apparatus which is intended to operate under internal pressure due to steam and belonging to or in the charge or under the control of the Insured.

It is obviously not the intention of the policy to provide cover in respect of damage to the insured's own property. This can be covered by various material damage policies and the insured cannot be legally liable for damage to his or her own property. For this reason it may seem that 2(a) of this exception is unnecessary but there are circumstances in which the owner of property loaned or hired to a third party may incur a liability for the cost of repairing that property if damaged while on hire. Taking the operative clause in isolation such an expense would be indemnified under the policy were it not for this exception.

It is not intended that the policy should cover property in the custody of control or the insured although there are circumstances in which the exception is amended or deleted in order to meet the requirements of an insured who may regularly have charge of customers' property for which a liability may be incurred in the event of loss or damage. Generally, however, such cover is available as part of or as an extension to material damage policies by means of an item covering "customers' goods held in trust" and it is preferable for businesses such as warehousekeepers, watch repairers and launderers, who are *bailees* of their customers' property, to obtain the necessary cover in this way. Most liability insurers are, however, prepared to cover risks such as cloakroom or car park liability.

It is not the purpose of this book to give detailed comments on the areas of law for which the public liability policy provides an indemnity unless such comments assist in the understanding of the policy but it is appropriate at this point to discuss, albeit briefly, the law relating to bailment.

There are two types of bailee: gratuitous bailees and bailees for reward. A bailee is a person who has custody of the property of another on the understanding that the property will be returned to its owner. The principal difference between the two classes of bailee is that a gratuitous bailee usually gains no benefit from the transaction, whereas the bailee for reward receives a benefit, normally in the form of payment, either for carrying out some work on the property or for merely keeping it safe. Not surprisingly, the courts impose a higher duty of care on bailees for reward. Therefore, if bailees for reward are unable to return the goods entrusted to them they have to show that the failure was not the result of fault on their part – normally in an action for negligence the burden of proof rests on the plaintiff to show that the loss or damage was the result of the defendant's negligence. If bailees for reward are able to show, for example, that the customer's property was stolen as the result of a theft following forceable entry to the bailees' premises, which they could not have prevented by the taking of reasonable care, this will be sufficient defence to a claim by the customer. However, the liability under a bailment for reward is contractual as well as tortious and the terms of any written agreement between the parties will need to be considered.

There is usually no contract between the parties in the case of a gratuitous bailment because there has been no consideration and the duty imposed on a gratuitous bailee is normally expressed as the standard a reasonable person would adopt for the safety of his or her own property.

Once again many of the practical problems encountered with this exception concern the building trade. What is the position, for example, of a builder carrying out repairs and renovation within an existing property? If the property or its contents are damaged as a result of his or her negligence does this exception operate and thus deny him or her an indemnity? Claims arising in these circumstances can range from minor damage to furniture being moved around, to the destruction of the property by fire due to the careless use of a blowlamp.

Firstly it should be noted that the policy being used as an example for the purpose of this book is not suitable for a building contractor although it is probably true to say that some builders will have similar policies and will therefore find that they have insufficient cover. It is by no means certain that an insurer would maintain that the furniture damaged or the building burned down were in the charge or under the custody or control of the insured but, in view of the doubt and the exposure to a potentially very expensive claim, the exception under a contractor's liability policy should be amended as follows:

> . . . this exception shall not apply to . . . premises not owned or rented by the insured but temporarily occupied by the insured for the purposes of alteration or repair there of or therein.

The exception does not apply to employees of the insured, but why is this if Exception 1 specifically excludes liability in respect of injury to employees? In other words, why should the policy deal with claims for employees' property if it does not provide cover for personal injury, particularly when there may be claims for both arising out of the same incident? In fact employees' effects are not considered to be in the employer's custody or control and employers' liability policies only cover bodily injury or disease although, in practice, the employers' liability insurer will deal with a claim for damage to clothing if included as an item of special damages as part of a claim for injury.

The reference to employees' property is therefore included to cover any gap between the two policies but in what circumstances would an employer be liable for loss or damage to employees' clothing and effects at the place of work?

In the case of *Deyong v Shenburn* (1946) it was held that,

(a) there was no implied term in the contract of employment that the employer would use all reasonable care in safeguarding the employee's property and
(b) the employer was under no duty of care, by virtue of the master and servant relationship, to take reasonable care to protect the property from theft.

There is therefore no special duty imposed on employers but they will be liable for loss or damage caused by negligence, as for example in the case of damage to employees' cars caused by the release of paint spray or chemicals from a factory.

Part (c) of the exception deals with particular types of plant and machinery but again only applies to damage to property. The historical reason for excluding these risks was that they were covered by engineering policies and the engineering departments of insurers were (and still are) responsible for carrying out regular inspections of such plant and machinery. However, public liability policies have gradually expanded to cover the liabilities arising from the ownership, possession and use of most types of plant and equipment and this exception is frequently omitted.

3. Liability in respect of injury loss or damage caused by or through or in connection with:

(a) Any passenger lift passenger elevator or passenger escalator owned by or in the possession of the Insured. This Exception shall not apply in respect of the occasional carriage of passengers on any goods lift goods elevator or goods escalator.

Exception 3(a) also deals with risks which can be covered by more specific policies and, like 2(c) above, 3(a) is included because the risks relating to lifts and elevators are covered by engineering policies.

Why then are lifts and elevators treated separately and not simply added as part of the previous exception? The reason is that this exception applies to injury as well as loss and damage to property. The exception only applies to passenger lifts and elevators and it would seem to be principally the risk of injury to users that insurers are anxious to exclude as there is a history of a high frequency of claims, a substantial proportion of which involve serious injury. The exception does not therefore apply to the occasional use by passengers of lifts and elevators used for the carriage of goods. However, the way in which this exception is worded would also exclude any claim arising as a result of an electrical fault leading to a fire which damages third party property. As with the previous exception the modern practice is for this exception to be omitted and for third party elevator and lift risks to be covered under the public liability policy.

> (b) The ownership or possession or use by or on behalf of the Insured of:
> (i) any vehicle (or machine) which is capable of self-propulsion or attached to a self-propelled vehicle and used in circumstances to which the Road Traffic Acts apply; or
> (ii) any vehicle (or machine) which is insured for the benefit of the Insured under any form of Motor Insurance Policy; or
> (iii) any vessel or craft not specified in the Schedule under the heading of Plant.

The following definition appears at the end of the Exceptions section:

> In these exceptions the expression "vessel or craft" shall include any vessel craft or thing made or intended to float on or in or travel on or through water or air.

It is not the intention of the public liability policy to cover vehicles or plant insured under a motor policy or the use of any mechanically propelled vehicles in circumstances in which the Road Traffic Acts apply. Third party risks associated with vehicles and plant are covered by motor insurance.

Marine and aviation insurance deals with transport by water and air and therefore loss, injury and damage arising out of the use of vessels and craft as defined are also excluded.

Certain problems can arise when there is doubt about whether a vehicle is used in circumstances to which the Road Traffic Acts apply and where there is no motor insurance policy in force.

On large construction sites, for example, access to different areas of the site may be by means of private site roads or public roads and the contractor will be using vehicles as well as construction plant such as excavators and dumpers. What then is the situation if a van belonging to the contractor, registered for road use and insured under a motor policy injures a member of the public who is lawfully using one of the private site roads? Clearly subsection (ii) of the exception would apply and the policy would not operate. But, if the same vehicle was not insured we would need to refer to subsection (i) and consider whether the van was being

Exceptions – risks covered by other policies

used in circumstances to which the Road Traffic Acts apply. In fact, if the Acts apply there must be third party motor insurance in force but does the use of a van on a private site road come within the requirements of the Acts? If not then the policy will operate.

Part 6 of the Road Traffic Act 1972 deals with compulsory third party motor insurance and s. 143 requires that

> it shall not be lawful for a person to use, or to cause or permit any other person to use, a motor vehicle on a road unless there is in force in relation to the use of the vehicle by that person or that other person, as the case may be such a policy of insurance or such a security in respect of third party risks as complies with the requirements of this Part of this Act. . . .

In this context road means any road to which the public has access and would not therefore include a private road within the construction site.

There are a number of reported cases dealing with the definition of "road" as intended by the Road Traffic Acts and it seems that the fact that a right of way is private does not prevent it from coming within the provisions of the Acts. If it can be shown as a fact that the public has access to the right of way and that it would be considered as a road in the ordinary sense of the word, ie a definable way between two points over which vehicles can pass, then the right of way is a road for the purposes of the Road Traffic Acts and Regulations (*Oxford v Austin* (1981)).

Any vehicle which is not licensed for road use and not covered by a motor policy is covered by the public liability policy and this would include all vehicles and mechanical plant used solely on the site of any contract works or within a factory premises.

What then is the situation of a vehicle which, although not registered for road use and not covered by a motor policy, is driven for a short distance along a public road while travelling between two separate parts of a site or factory? Any accident arising in these circumstances would not be covered by the policy as the vehicle is being used in circumstances to which the Road Traffic Acts apply even though the owner is in breach of the Acts by not having the required insurance.

As use in circumstances to which the Road Traffic Acts apply and use where third party motor insurance is required amount to the same thing many policies simply exclude

> motor vehicles which are licensed for road use or for which a certificate of motor insurance is required, or not used only on premises of the insured or on sites to which the public has no general right of access.

Because the exception refers to

> damage caused by or through or *in connection with* . . . the ownership or possession or use by or on behalf of the Insured of . . . any vehicle (or machine) which is insured for the benefit of the Insured under any form of Motor Insurance Policy. . . .

there can be problems in the event of accidents occurring whilst such a vehicle or machine is being loaded or unloaded. The motor policy normally excludes injury or damage arising from such operations, carried out by any person other than the driver or attendant of the vehicle, when they take place away from public roads and the public liability policy covers this liability. However to make the position quite clear some policies add the following clause:

> This policy is extended to indemnify the Insured in respect of liability for injury or damage caused or arising beyond the limits of any carriageway or thoroughfare in connection with (a) the bringing of the load to such vehicle for loading thereon: or (b) the taking away of the load from such vehicle after unloading by any person other than the driver or attendant of such vehicle.

This clause adequately covers any gap which there may be between the two policies because of the similar wording of the motor policy exception.

The liability policy usually covers what is known as the "tool of trade risk" which is generally excluded by the motor policy. This refers to the risk of injury or damage being caused during the use of mechanical plant for the purpose for which it was intended rather than movement under its own power from one place to another, eg an excavator bucket damaging an underground cable or a crane hitting an overhead cable. It is important that the insured using such equipment ensures that, if this risk is excluded from the motor policy, the liability policy affords the necessary cover.

As the exception refers to ownership, possession or use by or on behalf of the insured it does not apply to the situation where an accident occurs because of the misdirection by the insured or his employees of another party's vehicle, or the negligent loading or unloading of such a vehicle by the insured.

The reference in 3(b)(iii) to vessels or craft is included so as to allow provision for cover to be provided for small watercraft, barges and pontoons used by contractors so long as they are specified in the Schedule.

The sub-clauses 3(c) and (d), which refer to professional advice and goods sold, are also exceptions in respect of risks which are covered by more specific policies but require separate attention and will be considered in detail in the next chapter.

(e) The ownership or tenure by the Insured of any land or building not specified in the Schedule under the heading The Premises.

This clause only concerns liability in respect of the *ownership or tenure* of land or buildings and does not therefore apply to all accidents on premises not specified. Liability incurred as a result of accidents occurring at or on premises which the insured does not own or have any tenancy agreement in are covered.

Under The Defective Premises Act 1972 liabilities might arise out of premises which the insured has disposed of and which are not specified in the Schedule.

S. 3 of the Act includes the following provision:

> Where work of construction, repair, maintenance or demolition or any other work is done on or in relation to premises, any duty of care owed, because of the doing of the work, to persons who might reasonably be expected to be affected by the defects in the state of the premises created by the doing of the work shall not be abated by the subsequent disposal of the premises by the person who owed the duty.

To deal with this potential liability in respect of property no longer owned or occupied by the insured the following, or similar, clause may be added to the policy:

> The indemnity provided by this policy shall also apply to legal liabilities incurred by the Insured by virtue of section 3 of the Defective Premises Act 1972 in connection with premises which have been disposed of by the Insured. The Company shall not be liable; (a) for the cost of remedying any defect or alleged defect in the premises disposed of; (b) if the Insured is entitled to indemnity from any other policy.

This cover only remains in force during the currency of the policy and applies to accidents occurring during the policy period (see comments on Operative Clause) even though the defects may have arisen during an earlier period. Of course if, because of the nature of the insured's business, there is a higher than normal risk of liabilities being incurred under this Act, special consideration will be required and the insured would have to declare any defects of which he or she was aware.

CHAPTER 6

Exceptions – risks covered by other policies (continued) – product liability and professional indemnity insurance

As mentioned in the previous chapter it is appropriate to consider exceptions 3(c) and (d) separately from the other parts of exception 3 as they concern matters which are dealt with by policies covering product liability and professional negligence, both of which, although not topics to be covered in detail by this text, require some comment.

> Exception 3. Liability in respect of injury loss or damage caused by or through or in connection with:
> (c) Remedial or professional or other advice or treatment (other than medical first aid treatment) given or administered or omitted by the Insured.
> (d) Any goods or any container thereof sold or supplied or repaired or renovated or let on hire or handled by the Insured and no longer in the Insured's custody or control.

First Aid

Exception 3(c) does not apply to first aid treatment as it is not intended to exclude liability in respect of injury or damage arising out of treatment given by any first aid facility provided by the insured for dealing with emergencies or giving minor treatment resulting from accidents on their premises.

Advice

The potential claims associated with the giving of advice, in a professional capacity or otherwise, are such that the provision of the necessary insurance is not a matter for the public liability policy and professions such as architects, surveyors, accountants and solicitors obtain professional indemnity insurance, often through special schemes arranged by their professional associations.

In Chapter 3 reference was made to *Hedley Byrne and Co Ltd v Heller and Partners Ltd* (1964) and it is this case which, perhaps more than any other, has had a major effect on the law relating to liability for negligent statements and advice, and hence also on liability insurance. Before this case it was thought that the liability of a professional person was limited to those he or she was directly advising, ie clients with whom there was a contractual relationship. If some other party, not in a contractual or fiduciary (eg trustee/beneficiary) relationship, suffered loss as a result of the negligent advice he or she had no legal remedy, as it was considered that the professional owed him or her no duty of care.

Although in the *Hedley Byrne* case it was held that no duty of care was owed by the defendants in the particular circumstances of that case the judgements made it clear that such a duty could arise for negligent statements even in the absence of a contractual or fiduciary relationship between the parties. In his judgement Lord Morris of Borth-y-Gest said:

> . . . I consider that it follows and that it should now be regarded as settled that if someone possessed of a special skill undertakes, quite irrespective of contract, to apply that skill for the assistance of another person who relies on such skill, a duty of care will arise. The fact that the service is to be given by means of, or by the instrumentality of, words can make no difference. Furthermore, if, in a sphere in which a person is so placed that others could reasonably rely on his judgment or his skill or on his ability to make careful inquiry, a person takes it on himself to give information or advice to, or allows his information or advice to be passed on to, another person who, as he knows or should know, will place reliance on it, then a duty of care will arise.

This case has placed greater significance on the exception without which the insurer would now be exposed to many more claims than the exception was intended to avoid when originally drafted.

In addition to the professions this exception is also relevant to any company which provides advice on how to use its products. Again, professional indemnity insurance would be more appropriate but cover for advice given in connection with the supply or sale of a product is normally covered by the product liability policy unless such advice is given for a fee.

Professional indemnity

The professional indemnity policy follows the basic framework of the public liability policy but indemnifies the insured against *claims made* during the policy period for damages and claimants' costs for breach of professional duty due to negligent act, error or omission. It is important to note that the policy indemnifies in respect of error, omission or negligent acts and not merely a breach of warranty or contract, and that the negligence must have been committed in the conduct of the business.

Professional indemnity cover is on a "claims made" (see Chapter 3) basis but there is usually a restriction on retrospective cover by excluding claims due to negligence occurring a fixed period before inception of the policy. Although the proposer for professional indemnity is under a duty to disclose material facts it is normal for the proposal form to seek information about earlier occurrences likely to give rise to claims so that the underwriter can make further enquiries and exclude these if necessary.

In the event of cover lapsing insurers are usually willing to treat claims notified within three months, and resulting from negligent acts before cancellation, as though they had been notified during the policy period, although this extension is not available if the cover has been transferred to another insurer.

As with the public liability policy cover includes the payment of costs and expenses incurred with insurer's consent although, where the claim exceeds the limit of indemnity, the costs paid will be limited to that proportion of the costs that the limit of indemnity bears to the amount paid or payable.

Limit of indemnity

Unlike the public liability policy the limit of indemnity is in respect of any one occurrence. It includes damages and claimant's costs and expenses but not the insured's own costs and can be reinstated if the limit is eroded by several claims.

The professional indemnity policy can be extended to cover libel and slander, breach of warranty of authority (where an agent acting on behalf of a principal exceeds his or her other authority) dishonest, fraudulent, criminal or malicious act or omission of employees or agents, and loss of documents deposited with the insured.

> Exception 3 Liability in respect of injury loss or damage caused by or through or in connection with:
> (d) Any goods or any container thereof sold or supplied or repaired or renovated or let on hire or handled by the Insured and no longer in the Insured's custody or control.

Product liability

The product liability risk is also catered for by a separate policy and gives rise to an ever increasing number of claims principally because of the increased awareness of the public through various consumer organisations and pressure groups and consumer/sale of goods legislation. However, the most expensive and complex claims generally arise from dealings between commercial organisations which can give rise to claims for damage and lost production as a result of the supply of faulty raw materials by one company to be incorporated into another company's product. Many companies can be involved in a chain of supply before the product reaches the final consumer. This is therefore a potential liability which requires separate consideration although it is common nowadays for combined public and products liability policies to be issued.

Containers

This exception applies to the containers as well as the goods supplied and would therefore apply to any accident arising out of defective packaging or incorrect labelling. It does not, however, apply to the goods or their containers until they have left the insured's custody and control. Therefore, any damage or injury caused to third parties by the goods while still in the insured's custody or control, such as leakage or escape of dangerous chemicals, would be covered.

In possession of insured or customer

Confusion can arise with this wording in the case of goods which have left the insured's premises but have not come into the possession of the customer. For example the insured's employee may have left goods outside a customer's premises for collection in such a position that an accident is caused. Such an accident has been caused by or in connection with goods sold and should be excluded, but most insurers would deal with the claim as it is their intention to exclude claims arising from the nature or character of these goods and not the negligence of an employee in placing them in a dangerous position. However if, because of some dangerous property of the goods and insecure packing, the same goods exploded causing extensive damage and injury, the policy exception would be applied. To avoid any confusion the wording may be amended to read: "Liability arising out of the nature or condition of any goods sold or supplied . . .".

Food, drink and refreshments

Many businesses provide canteen facilities for their staff and visitors and this exception is usually altered so that the policy covers claims arising from food, drink and refreshments sold or supplied at such establishments but only so long as this facility is ancillary to the main business. If catering forms a substantial part of the business special considerations will apply and a separate policy may be required.

Goods repaired or renovated

As well as goods sold or supplied the exception applies to customers goods which have been repaired, renovated, or handled by the insured. If, for example, an electric motor has been renovated and rewound by the insured and causes a fire at the customer's premises because of faulty workmanship by the insured the claim will not be met because of this exception. But what is the situation if the same motor had been repaired by the insured, without the supply of any new parts, at the customer's premises? In view of the *contra proferentem* rule by which the clause in dispute would be interpreted against the insurer and the requirement that the onus is on the insurer to prove that the exception applies, it is probable that the public liability policy would have to deal with this. The inclusion of the words "no longer in the Insured's possession or control" would suggest that it is intended that the exception only applies to goods which have been at the insured's premises.

There are many different wordings used for this exception and each requires careful consideration as there are circumstances where a claim may be excluded by the public liability policy and also fall outside the cover granted under the product liability policy.

It is therefore appropriate to consider the product liability policy at this point.

Product liability policy

The policy follows the same basic format as the public liability policy and indemnifies the insured in respect of legal liability to pay damages and claimants' costs in respect of accidental bodily injury and accidental damage to material property occurring during the period of insurance and caused by or arising out of products (including containers, labelling, instructions, or advice provided in connection therewith) sold, supplied, erected, repaired, altered, treated or installed by the insured in connection with the business. It is not usual to cover financial loss which is not consequent upon injury or loss of or damage to property, although cover can be provided at extra cost.

Location of injury or damage

The injury or damage may occur anywhere in the world, other than at premises owned or occupied by the insured, but the policy is usually restricted to goods sold or supplied, etc from premises in Great Britain, Northern Ireland, the Channel Islands or the Isle of Man, or countries within the EC. The limit of indemnity applies to any one period of insurance but can be reinstated if eroded by a claim or claims within the period.

Goods sold or supplied

The "goods sold or supplied" exception in the public liability policy does not only apply to retailers, suppliers and manufacturers as it refers to "any goods . . . repaired or renovated . . . or handled by the insured". The word "handled" is rather vague and many policies use terms such as "serviced", "treated" and "altered". Whatever form of words is used it is essential that the operative clause of the product public liability policy is worded so that there is no gap between it and the public liability policy. This should not happen if a combined policy is issued and nowadays this is normal practice. This is achieved either by having a single policy with separate sections covering public liability, employers' liability and product liability or by a combined public/product liability policy with a single operative clause. Alternatively, a public liability policy may be extended by endorsement to cover the product liability risk.

Probably the two most important points to remember about the product liability policy are that it *does not cover*:

(a) the cost of replacement, recall, reinstatement or repair of the goods sold or supplied, or;
(b) any claim resulting from the failure of the product to perform its intended function.

It is these two points that cause most problems in the handling of claims because the cost of replacement or recall could represent a substantial uninsured loss to the insured, and because it could be a matter of opinion as to whether a claim arises because a product has failed to perform due to its unsuitability as against its simply being defective. The following examples may help explain the problem.

(a) A manufacturer of printing inks and varnishes advises a customer that a certain varnish will be suitable for the customer's particular requirements. The varnish is one of the manufacturer's standard products and can be supplied to this customer without any modification. The customer uses the varnish to print advertising material for his customers and finds that he is not able to achieve the quality of finish that he had been led to expect by the varnish manufacturer. He lodges a claim for the value of labour and materials (including the cost of the varnish) used and for loss of profit due to cancellation of the order by his customer.

The varnish manufacturer looks to his product liability policy for an indemnity. In response, and this depends on the exact policy wording, most insurers would say that the claim has not arisen because of any defect in the product which has caused damage to third party property, but that the product was exactly what the insured intended to supply and the claim has arisen because it was not suitable for the intended purpose. The manufacturer, who may be faced with a claim for many thousands of pounds, argues that the claim has arisen because he gave the wrong advice in connection with the product and that there has been damage to third party property, namely the loss of the materials used in the printing. Some insurers would accept this as a valid claim, as long as the advice had not been given for a fee separate from the cost of the product, but the value of the varnish would be excluded. The claim for loss of profit sustained by the insured's customer would also be covered if the insured were legally liable for that item of the claim.

If the printer had tested the varnish and discovered that it was not suitable before he used it in production, any claim for financial loss would not be covered because of the absence of loss or damage.

(b) A manufacturer of aluminium window frames supplies frames to a builder for incorporation into a new building and, following completion of the building it is discovered that there are faults in the frames which, although causing no damage, are not acceptable to the architect who instructs the builder to remove and replace the frames. The builder makes a claim against the manufacturer for the expense incurred.

As there has been no damage to any property other than the frames this is not a matter for the policy which, in any event, specifically excludes the cost of replacing the product itself whether that cost is incurred by the insured or by others.

The exception dealing with cost of replacement and repair should be worded so that it does not apply to work done or goods supplied by the insured under a separate contract, eg while installing a machine at a customer's factory a machine supplied by the insured at an earlier date is damaged because of a defect in the new machine or because of the negligence of the insured's employees.

It has already been seen that there are occasions when it is difficult to determine whether a claim is a public or product liability matter and many such problems arise in connection with repairs or servicing. This is well illustrated by the case of *Wayne Tank and Pump Co Ltd v Employers' Liability Assurance Corporation Ltd* (1973).

A fire occurred on the night of 5.2.63 at the premises of Harbutt's Plasticine Ltd at Bathampton, Somerset as a result of which the factory was destroyed. Harbutts alleged that the fire started because of the faulty installation and operation of equipment supplied by Wayne Tank. Legal action was successful and Wayne Tank sought an indemnity under its public liability policy with Employers' Liability Assurance Corporation.

The insurer did not think that its policy applied as it contained an exception under the terms of which it was not liable to indemnify the insured in respect of "damage caused by the nature of goods sold or supplied by the insured". The dispute eventually came before the Court of Appeal where the main argument centred around the question of whether the fire had been caused by the defective and dangerous installation, which was not in dispute, or the negligent action of an employee of Wayne Tank who had left a heating appliance, which formed part of the installation, switched on and unattended overnight. If the defective installation were the proximate cause of the fire, then insurers were protected by the exception, but if the proximate cause was the action of the employee they were not and so would be liable.

Lord Denning held that the proximate cause was the defective installation. He rejected the argument that the "last cause" (the employee's action) alone should be looked at, and said that, of the two causes the defective installation was the dominant cause and that the employee's action in switching on the heater was not one which broke the chain of causation between the supply of the defective machinery and the fire. He also stated that even if he were wrong about this, and the two causes were equal or nearly equal in bringing about the fire, the insurer was still entitled to the benefit of the exception clause, even if only one of the causes fell within the terms.

In delivering his judgement Lord Denning drew attention to an important rule regarding the interpretation of insurance contracts by stating:

> Although the accident might be within the general words at the opening of the policy, nevertheless when there was a particular exception, the particular words took priority over the general words. General words always gave way to a particular provision. So if the case came within the particular exception, the exception prevailed. The accident came within the particular words of the exception; it was caused by the nature or condition of the goods supplied.

Lord Denning's judgement gives useful guidance on the intepretation of exception clauses. It seems that, in cases where servicing or installation work is being carried out at a customer's premises, any loss or damage caused as the direct and sole result of the method of work or the negligent actions of workers should be dealt with by the public liability policy and any loss or damage directly caused by the defective goods is a matter for the product liability policy. This would include any defect in the goods caused by the workers at the time of installation as well as defects arising at the time of manufacture prior to delivery to the customer.

CHAPTER 7

Exceptions – risks outside the scope of the policy – uninsurable risks – excess clause

There is only one exception which would be considered as relating to a risk which is outside the scope of the policy under consideration and it deals with liabilities which the insured may assume under contract with other parties.

> 4. Liability assumed by the Insured by agreement unless such liability would have attached to the Insured notwithstanding such agreement.

Insurers do not intend to cover any liabilities which the insured may incur because of the terms of contracts or agreements with third parties and this exception is intended to exclude all such contractual liabilities. The policy is intended to cover the insured's legal liability in tort and insurers are unwilling to extend this to include what may be very onerous contractual liabilities unless they have full knowledge of the type of contract involved in order to assess the risk and charge the appropriate premium. There are many "standard" forms of contract, particularly those used in the construction industry, and most insurers are prepared to give contractual liability cover in respect of such contracts where the insured is regularly carrying on business under such contracts. Most forms of building contract, for example, require the contractor to indemnify the principal in respect of injury to third parties and damage to third party property and this would be catered for either by special endorsement extending the policy cover or by amending the exception as follows:

> Subject otherwise to its terms and conditions the exception of liability assumed by agreement shall not include liability which arises under an indemnity given by the Insured to the principal for which the insured is carrying out work in connection with the Business.

Contractual liabilities range from those which are merely a restatement of liabilities which would in any event arise in tort to those requiring the payment of liquidated damages if the contract is not completed within the required time. The exception makes it clear that liabilities which would have arisen outside the specific contract terms are not excluded and, as seen above, insurers are prepared to cover certain other liabilities: they are not however prepared to cover contractual liabilities for such as liquidated damages (the value of which has probably been set by the principal and is payable at a weekly/monthly rate in the event of delay or other default by the supplier/contractor) or other liabilities which are not covered by the operative clause of the policy.

Exceptions relating to risks which are uninsurable

> 5. Any legal liability of whatsoever nature directly or indirectly caused by or contributed to by or arising from ionising radiations or contamination by radioactivity from any nuclear fuel or from any nuclear waste from the combustion of nuclear fuel.
> 6. Liability for any consequence of war invasion act of foreign enemy hostilities (whether war be declared or not) civil war rebellion revolution insurrection or military or usurped power.

These exceptions (or similarly worded ones) are common to all policies as the risks listed are unsuitable for commercial insurance. War risks are matters for the Government and radiation and contamination risks are matters for which the licensed nuclear power station operator concerned is strictly liable by statute (The Nuclear Installations Act 1965). S. 27 of the Energy Act 1983 increased the licensed operator's liability from £5,000,000 to £20,000,000 per incident; the total amount of compensation to be provided in respect of a nuclear incident by the operator and public funds together was increased from £50,000,000 per incident to approximately £210,000,000.

Excess clause

Although not itemised as a policy exception most liability policies are subject to an excess which is usually referred to in the schedule under a heading such as "Insured's retained liability".

The insured is responsible for a stated amount of each and every claim

Exceptions – risks outside the scope of the policy

but the wording of the clause should be such that it does not give rise to conflict or confusion with the proviso clause in the event of multiple claims arising out of one occurrence.

It would not be right for insurers to say that the limit of liability applied once to all claims arising out of one occurrence and at the same time apply separate excesses to the claims of individual claimants arising from that occurrence. This could arise if the excess clause referred to "each and every claim" whereas the proviso clause referred to the limit of indemnity applying to all claims arising out of one occurrence or accident. It may be the insurer's intention to apply excesses to each claim even if they do arise from one event, but that intention should be made clear by defining what is meant by words such as "occurrence", "claim", "event" and "any one accident".

The case of *South Staffordshire Tramways v Sickness and Accident Assurance (1891)* concerned a dispute over the number of excesses to be applied following an accident involving a tram car.

The policy stated that the plaintiffs would be provided with indemnity against all claims for personal injury, made against them in respect of "accidents caused by vehicles" belonging to them. One of their tram cars overturned and 40 people were injured.

It was held that this represented 40 claims and that 40 deductibles should apply. The reason given for this decision was that the accidents were caused by the vehicle and were therefore accidents to the individuals injured rather than an accident to the tram car of which there was only one.

Obviously the wording of the policy has to be considered in each case but it seems that the court reached this decision by looking at the incident from the point of view of the claimants. It is therefore interesting to contrast this with the more recent case *Forney v Dominion Insurance Company Limited* (1969) in which the court took the view that "occurrence" should be looked at from the insured's point of view, which does seem to be more sensible as the indemnity under the policy is for the benefit of the insured and the courts have tended to interpret words such as "accidental" by looking at them from the insured's point of view rather than the insurer's or the claimant's.

This case involved a claim under a solicitor's professional indemnity policy. A solicitor's clerk was dealing with legal matters resulting from a motor accident in which the driver had been killed and three of the passengers, including the driver's wife, were injured. The clerk negligently took out a grant of administration in the wife's name thus precluding her from suing her husband's estate (and its insurers) for the loss of her husband. The mistake was not rectified within the time allowed and, furthermore, the clerk failed to issue writs on behalf of the three injured passengers within the limitation period. Claims against the solicitor were settled by him and the question arose as to how many deductibles he would have to bear and how much he could claim under the policy.

The solicitor maintained that there was one occurrence, namely the mishandling of the matter as a whole. The insurer argued that there were a number of occurrences comprising the individual losses of each of the passengers and the widow's claim for the loss of her husband. The court found that there were two occurrences:

(a) the negligent obtaining of a grant of administration in the wife's name and,
(b) the untimely issuing of the writs.

The reason for this was that the two occurrences were different both in nature and chronology and the policy contained the phrase ". . . any one claim or number of claims arising out of the same occurrence . . .". The policy under consideration contained a proviso which limited the indemnity and contemplated the possibility that a number of claims may arise out of one occurrence. This seems to indicate that a number of persons may be injured by a single act of negligence of the insured and that occurrence in this context is looked at from the point of view of the insured. For this reason the court did not consider that the claims from the three passengers were separate occurrences or accidents.

Seen from the perspective of the insured the participation in losses by means of a deductible or excess is a way of saving premiums. The insured willingly foregoes cover in an area of minor significance where, due to the limited risk and its possible anticipation, he or she can make appropriate separate provisions to secure his or her own interests.

Seen from the perspective of the insurer such a participation in losses by the insured serves various purposes:

(a) it should eliminate the claims experience and administrative costs of dealing with small losses and
(b) it should encourage the insured to prevent losses in the first place and, where a loss has occurred, to assist in averting its consequences.

Excesses and deductibles are typically applied in circumstances where there has been experience of numerous minor thefts or damage such as on building sites. Contractors' public liability policies frequently include an excess, sometimes as much as £2500, in respect of damage to underground services, as well as a separate excess (not usually applicable to personal injury claims) for general third party claims. Practice varies amongst insurers as to how the excess is collected and, where it represents a significance proportion of the claim, the insurer should involve the insured closely in the handling of the claim. Depending on the amount involved the insurer may pay to the insured the agreed settlement figure, less the excess, leaving the insured to settle with the claimant (see *Hayler v Chapman*, Chapter 8). However, if the excess is only a small proportion of the settlement the insurer should collect the excess from the insured before settling the claim with the third party.

The "settlement" to which the excess applies may take into account the legal costs incurred by the insurer, so that, if a third party claim were to be successfully defended without any payment being made to the third party, the excess would still be payable if the insurer had incurred legal costs in dealing with the claim.

As mentioned in Chapter 4, in the event that the excess forms a substantial part of the claim, agreement may be reached between insured and insurer to share the legal costs on a *pro rata* basis.

In practice the exact basis on which the excess is applied is not normally adequately defined. An excess clause such as "The Insured shall bear the first £** of each and every claim in respect of loss of or damage to property" may appear on the policy schedule without any further definition elsewhere in the policy. It is submitted that in this case the excess would apply to any claim as defined in the proviso clause (damages payable to any claimant) which falls within the limit of indemnity and that, as costs are paid in addition to the limit of indemnity, no excess should be collected in the event that there is no payment of damages to the third party even if costs are incurred by the insurer.

The sample excess clause above refers to property damage and it is normal for insurers not to apply any excess to injury claims in order that they can retain full control over the handling of such claims.

CHAPTER 8

Policy conditions

Conditions come into two broad categories, those that are implied and others that are express conditions.

Implied conditions

Implied conditions are those that are common to all contracts of insurance, eg:

(a) the parties shall observe good faith towards each other at all material times and in all material particulars;
(b) that there is a subject matter of insurance in existence at the time when the policy is effective;
(c) that the subject matter of insurance is so described in the policy as clearly to identify it and to define the risk undertaken by the insurers and;
(d) that the insured has an insurable interest in the subject matter of the insurance.

It is the practice of insurers to insert in their policies express conditions which may extend or restrict the scope of the implied conditions.

The conditions may be further classified into three types by reference to the time when they come into operation:

(a) conditions precedent to the validity of the policy,
(b) conditions subsequent to the policy and,
(c) conditions precedent to the liability of insurers.

A condition precedent relates to matters which precede the formation of the contract contained in the policy and are generally essential to the validity of the policy, otherwise the policy is void from inception. For example, it is, or may be, a condition precedent that the insured shall discharge his or her duty of disclosure and that all statements made during the negotiations by the insured shall be true. Therefore, if a shopkeeper states that no claims have been made against him by customers being injured in his shop but is aware that there have in fact been several complaints and claims from people slipping on a defective floor, the policy is void.

Conditions subsequent

Conditions subsequent relate to matters which arise after the formation of the contract and a breach will render the policy void from the date of the breach. If, in the previous example, the shopkeeper revealed all information about previous claims but later failed to advise insurers that he was expanding his business to provide a home maintenance service where employees would be working away from the shop premises, the policy would be voidable at the option of the insurer from the date on which the new business commenced and it would not be liable to deal with any claims arising from the new business.

Conditions precedent

Conditions precedent to liability relate to matters arising after an incident which leads to a claim being made under the policy and define the circumstances in which the liability of insurers is to arise. Such conditions must be fulfilled otherwise the insurers can avoid liability for that particular loss. If the shopkeeper already referred to receives a claim from a customer whose carpet has been ruined by paint spilled by one of his employees carrying out maintenance work and he decides to pay for a replacement and then makes a claim on his liability policy, insurers would be entitled to repudiate the claim because of the breach of the condition requiring the policyholder not to nogotiate, admit liability or make any payment without the insurer's consent.

All conditions of the public liability policy are preceded by the following explanatory paragraph which makes it clear that all parts of the policy are to be read together and avoids the need for specific meanings or definitions of words and phrases to be repeated:

> This Policy and the Schedule shall be read together as one contract and any word or expression to which a specific meaning has been attached in any part of

this Policy or of the Schedule shall bear such specific meaning wherever it may appear.

The first condition of the policy is a condition precedent to liability and deals with notifications of claims or circumstances likely to give rise to claims:

> 1. The Insured shall give written notice to the Head Office or Branch Office of the Company of any injury loss or damage or claim or proceedings immediately the same shall have come to the knowledge of the Insured or his representative.

It is most important that the insurer is told about incidents involving injury, loss or damage as soon as possible so that they can investigate and take whatever action may be necessary to protect their position. Insurers normally take a reasonable attitude and would not rely on a breach of this condition to avoid dealing with the claim unless it was clear that they had been prejudiced by the delay. The difficulty for the insured is that a very minor incident, which might not seem worth reporting at the time, could later develop into a claim, by which time the scene of the accident may have changed and important witnesses might no longer be available. Again, insurers tend to be sympathetic in these circumstances but it is best for all incidents, however minor, to be reported so that the insurers can then decide what action to take. If the insurers decide not to investigate then they cannot rely on breach of the condition at a later date.

Late notification

In the event of late notification insurers would normally agree to investigate but they should ensure that the insured is aware that such investigations are being carried out "without prejudice" to liability under the policy. If this is not made clear insurers may find that, by conducting enquires and taking any action in response to a claim from the insured when there has been a clear breach of policy condition, they are prevented (estopped) from relying on the condition.

The condition can be amended to permit reporting of incidents to brokers or other authorised agents of the insurer.

Conduct of insured and insurer in negotiations claims

> 2. The Insured shall not without the consent in writing of the Company repudiate liability negotiate or make any admission offer promise or payment

in connection with any injury loss or damage or claim and the Company shall be entitled if it so desires to take over and conduct in the name of the Insured the defence of any claim or to prosecute in the name of the Insured at its own expense and for its own benefit any claim for indemnity or damages or otherwise against any persons and shall have full discretion in the conduct of any proceedings and in the settlement of any claim and the Insured shall give all such information and assistance as the Company may require.

This condition deals with the conduct of the insured and insurer in the handling and negotiation of claims and makes it clear that insurers retain control of all claims and are entitled to conduct proceedings, either in defence or prosecution of claims, in the name of the insured.

As with Condition 1, it is very important that the insured immediately notifies the insurer of any claim, writ or correspondence received without making any response or acknowledgment to the other party.

It was previously mentioned, when discussing the policy excess, that there will be occasions when the insured could have a substantial interest in the outcome of the claim because of the size of the excess. It is possible that, in such circumstances, the insured might disagree with the way in which the insurer is conducting the claim. Nevertheless, if the insured wishes to obtain the benefit of the policy he or she would be bound by this condition but would always have the option of withdrawing the claim and dealing with it himself or herself if agreement could not be reached as to the way in which the claim should be handled.

Subrogation

The common law principle of subrogation, which is an implied condition of the contract, allows the insurer to pursue actions against other parties in the name of the insured but this only arises after the insured has been indemnified, and so the terms of this condition amend the common law principle.

The Court of Appeal considered the question of subrogation where there were insured and uninsured losses in the following case: *Hayler v Chapman* (1989).

On 12.12.84 there was a collision between two cars driven by the plaintiff and the defendant. Each party informed his own insurer; in the plaintiff's case, the Beacon and, in the defendant's case, the Halifax. The Beacon paid the plaintiff £775, being the write-off value of the car, and then sought to recover its outlay from the Halifax by way of subrogation.

The plaintiff, without informing his insurer, sought to recover his uninsured loss from the defendant's insurer. His claim was for car hire charges, the excess under his policy, phone calls and taxi fares. Meanwhile, the Beacon set out in a letter to the Halifax its claim for the amount paid to the plaintiff as well as for his uninsured loss. Halifax replied to the Beacon and to the plaintiff denying liability in each case.

On 7.6.85 the plaintiff started proceedings in the County Court and, on 27th August, was awarded £94.70, that judgement being satisfied by the Halifax.

On 26.6.86 the Beacon, which was clearly unaware of the plaintiff's claim and his proceedings, instructed its solicitors to send a letter before action to the Halifax, which replied, saying:

> We note the nature of the claim that you are instructed to pursue. This includes Hayler's personal claim. What you presumably do not know is that Hayler has already obtained judgement in the Bournemouth County Court. This judgement has been satisfied and as far as our understanding of the rules is concerned, no further action can be brought in Hayler's name subsequent to this particular accident.

Eventually, in May 1987, the Beacon launched their action and applied to have the plaintiff's judgement in the first proceedings set aside so that they could be amended to include a claim for the insured as well as the uninsured loss. The judge refused to set aside the award and it is this decision which was the subject of the appeal.

It was held that:

(a) before a court took the unusual step of setting aside a judgement given after a contested hearing there would have to be evidence as to the conduct of the parties showing that it was unjust and inequitable for the judgement to stand and thereby bar any additional claim;

(b) there was nothing in the evidence to show that the Halifax had acted so deliberately to exploit the misunderstanding between the plaintiff and the Beacon and the inferences which would be necessary to spell out any injustice or inequity were too numerous and speculative on the available evidence; the circumstances did not justify the setting aside of the award; the appeal would be dismissed.

This Court of Appeal case illustrates that care needs to be taken to protect insurers' rights of subrogation when the insured also wishes to recover uninsured losses.

It should be noted, however, that this decision would not allow an insurer on the receiving end of a recovery action to avoid payment of the pursuing insurer's outlay by quickly settling a claim for uninsured losses. In his judgement Lord Justice Taylor states:

> ... there is nothing to show that the Halifax acted so as deliberately to exploit the misunderstanding between the Beacon and the plaintiff, their insured. They did not, as happens in some reported cases, hasten to settle the plaintiff's small claim and then tell his insurers that their claim was barred ...

From the point of view of the insurer pursuing recovery it is evident that closer and more diligent contact with the insured at an early stage would avoid any such misunderstanding.

The insurer must bring the subrogation action in the name of the insured unless there has been an assignment and, if the insured company has been wound up prior to such an assignment, an action would be unable to proceed (*M H Smith (Plant Hire) Ltd v Mainwaring* (1986)).

The decision in *Petrofina (UK) Ltd v Magnaload* (1983) confirmed that it is not possible to bring an action against a joint insured.

Limit of liability

> 3. The Company may in the case of any injury loss or damage pay to the Insured the Limit of Indemnity for any one accident (but deducting therefrom in such case any sum or sums already paid as damages in respect thereof) or any lesser sum for which the claim or claims arising therefrom can be settled and the Company shall thereafter be under no further liability in respect of such injury loss or damage except for the payment of costs and expenses of litigation referred to on the first page of this Policy and specified in items (a) and (b) thereof incurred prior to the date of the payment of such Limit of Indemnity or such lesser sum.

This condition was referred to in Chapter 4 when discussing the limit of liability and it should also be read in conjunction with the clauses dealing with indemnity in respect of costs and expenses. It should be noted, however, that the clause does not only apply in circumstances where the limit of liability has been, or is likely to be exceeded. The words ". . . or any lesser sum for which the claim or claims arising therefrom can be settled . . ." would allow the insurer to make such a payment and be discharged from further liability under the policy in respect of that claim. It is possible that the claim may be only part of some complex litigation involving matters which are of no concern to the public liability insurers but which could have the effect of increasing the costs for the claim with which they are concerned. It would therefore be sensible for the insurers to pay to the insured the agreed value of the claim for which the policy does provide an indemnity and so avoid further legal costs. It would be necessary for insurers to obtain a suitable form of discharge from their insured.

Contribution

> 4. If at the time of any claim arising under this insurance there shall be any other insurance covering the same risk or part thereof the Company shall not be liable for more than its rateable proportion thereof.

The public liability policy is a contract of indemnity which means that, subject to policy limits and excesses, payment is limited to the insured's pecuniary loss in respect of liability to pay damages to third parties in accordance with the operative clause of the policy. The principle of indemnity was described by Brett, LJ in *Castellain v Preston* (1881):

> The very foundation in my opinion of every rule which has applied to insurance law is this, namely that the contract of insurance contained in a marine or fire policy is a contract of indemnity only, and this contract means that the assured because of a loss against which the policy has been made shall be fully indemnified but shall never be more than fully indemnified. This is the fundamental principle of insurance and if ever a proposition is put forward which is at variance with it, that is to say, which either will prevent the assured from obtaining a full indemnity or which will give the assured more than a full indemnity that proposition must certainly be wrong.

Although specific reference is made to marine and fire insurance the principle applies to liability policies as they are contracts of indemnity.

Indemnity, along with subrogation and contribution, is a common law principle which is an implied condition of insurance contracts unless modified by express written conditions and, as with Condition 2 which modifies the implied condition of subrogation (see page 76), Condition 4 alters the common law principle of contribution. In the absence of the written condition the insured would be able to obtain indemnity from one insurer leaving that insurer to recover from any other insurer covering the same liability.

The condition states that where there is any other insurance covering the same risk the company shall not be liable for more than its rateable proportion. The two policies must also cover the same interest, ie to indemnify the same insured for certain specified liabilities. It does not matter that one of the policies covers additional items as long as both cover the liability in respect of which a claim is being made.

The principle of contribution or "sharing" arises from the case of *Dearing v Earl of Winchelsea* (1787). This case did not involve insurance policies but sureties whereby two people had accepted responsibility to guarantee the payment of money to be paid by another party. The debt was not paid and the sureties were called upon to fulfil their guarantees. The case was essentially about the proportions of responsibility that lay with the two guarantors and it was held "that the sums in each instrument ascertain the proportion".

The practical application of the contribution condition is frequently complicated because not all policies use the same form of words. If two policies contain the condition given as an example above then, where the claim falls below the limit of liability of both policies, each will contribute half up to the lower limit of indemnity.

This is illustrated by the case *Commercial Union Assurance Co Ltd v Hayden* (1977) which seems to be the only authority on contribution under liability policies. The Commercial Union issued a public liability policy with a limit of indemnity of £100,000 and a Lloyd's syndicate (represented by Hayden) issued a policy covering the same interest but with a limit of £10,000. A third party claim was settled by Commercial Union for £4425. The contribution clause in both policies stated that, in the event of the existence of another policy covering the same risk, the insurer would not be liable for more than the rateable proportion.

In the High Court it was held that Commercial Union should pay 10/11 and Lloyd's 1/11, ie their rateable proportions of the total of the two limits of indemnity (£110,000). The Court of Appeal considered that this was wrong and that claims up to the lower limit (£10,000) should be shared equally, that is the apportionment should be on an independent liability basis.

Independent liability

The independent liability method can be described as:

> A method of establishing the amount of contribution between policies based on the ratio of the independent liabilities of the respective policies. The independent liability of a policy is the liability of that policy without regard to the existence of any other policies.

The following examples explain the application of this method.

Example 1
Policy A   Limit of Indemnity   £ 10,000
Policy B   Limit of Indemnity   £250,000
Claim £40,000
Independent liability of Policy A   £10,000
Independent liability of Policy B   £40,000
The policies contribute in the ratio 10,000:50,000 (Total independent liabilities)
Policy A   1/5 × £40,000 Pays £ 8,000
Policy B   4/5 × £40,000 Pays £32,000
Total Claim   £40,000

Example 2
Same policies as Example 1
Claim £300,000
Independent liability of Policy A   £ 10,000
Independent liability of Policy B   £250,000
The policies contribute in the ratio 10,000:260,000
Policy A   1/26 × £300,00 = £ 11,538
Limit of Indemnity is £10,000 and therefore Policy A pays £10,000
Policy B   25/26 × £300,000 = £288,462
Limit of Indemnity is £250,000 and therefore Policy A pays £250,000
Total paid by Policies A and B   £260,000
The balance of £40,000 is uninsured and is paid by the insured.

Example 3
Same policies as in Examples 1 and 2
Claim £5,000
Independent liability of Policy A   £5,000
Independent liability of Policy B   £5,000
The policies contribute in the ratio 5,000:10,000
Each policy therefore pays £2,500 and the claim is shared equally in accordance with the judgement in *Commercial Union Assurance v Hayden*.

As mentioned above not all policies use the same wording and may attempt to avoid contribution entirely using a clause such as:

> The Company is not to be called upon in contribution under the insurance and is only to pay any loss hereon in and so far as this is not otherwise recoverable under any other insurance.

Two motor policies containing non-contribution clauses were considered in *Gale v Motor Union Assurance Co Ltd* (1928): *Loyst v General Accident Fire and Life Assurance Corporation Ltd* (1928). Claims were made against both policies following an accident giving rise to a third party claim. Both insurers denied liability but it was held that each should contribute equally.

Claim investigation and cooperation

> 5. The Company may at all reasonable times for the purpose of enquiry or examination by their authorised officials and agents enter into any premises or places to which this insurance applies or in which injury loss or damage has occurred and may remain in possession for a reasonable period for the purpose of such enquiry or examination and the Insured shall give all necessary facilities in connection therewith.

It is very rarely that an insurer would need to rely on this condition but, as a condition precedent, lack of cooperation and breach of this condition by the insured would allow the insurer to refuse to deal with the claim. It also allows the insurer to use persons other than their direct employees for inspection of the places referred to in the condition. Many accidents occur away from the insured's own premises or other places under their control and this condition does not give insurers any right of entry to third party premises although the insured would be expected to provide assistance where possible to enable the insurer to get permission to enter such premises.

Reasonable care

> 6. The Insured shall exercise reasonable care in the selection of competent employees and shall take all reasonable precautions to prevent injury loss or damage.

This is a condition precedent to liability under the policy a breach of which will enable the insurer to refuse an indemnity in respect of the claim under consideration. It is probable that insurers attempt to enforce this condition more than any other, with the possible exception of the claim notification condition. However, the circumstances in which it is appropriate to do so are very limited, as will be seen.

The policy indemnifies the insured for, *inter alia*, the results of negligence and, recalling the definition of negligence, this means actions where there has been a breach of the duty of care. It would therefore make a nonsense of the policy if an insurer interpreted this condition literally and tried to avoid a claim because of lack of care on the part of the insured.

The two principle points requiring consideration are:

(a) what is meant by reasonable care/reasonable precautions and;
(b) what is meant by "the Insured"?

Firstly, it is useful to refer back to the discussion in Chapter 3 dealing with the meaning of "accidental" in the operative clause as it is clear that any actions considered to be "reckless" or "wilful" and carried out without regard for the consequences (*Filliter v Phippard* and *Fenton v Thorley*) would not be covered even if this clause was not present. But that is one extreme, so is there any degree of lack of care which falls between this extreme and the lack of care which the policy intends to cover?

Goddard LJ made known his views on this in the Court of Appeal case *Woolfall and Rimmer Limited v Moyle* (1941):

> If we were to read that condition in the way in which Counsel for the Appellants has invited us to read it, it seems to me that it would follow that the underwriters were saying "I will insure you against your liability for negligence on condition that you are not negligent" because if the employer has taken all reasonable precautions to prevent accidents it follows that he cannot be liable in negligence . . . I think that as soon as one remembers that what has to be construed is a contract between the insurers and the insured things become reasonably clear. It is a condition which is put in for the protection of the underwriter, or perhaps one might say, to limit the field of the underwriter's liability to the extent that he is saying: "I will insure you against the consequences of your negligence but understand that I am insuring you on the footing that you are not to regard yourself, because you are insured, as free to carry on your business in a reckless manner. You are to take those reasonable precautions to prevent accidents which ordinary business people take. That is to say you are to run your business in the ordinary way and not in a way which invites accidents".

In view of this judgement there is little doubt that insurers cannot expect to receive a very sympathetic response from the courts if they attempt to rely on this condition but it does still leave open the question of what is meant by "reasonable precautions to prevent accidents" and "not in a way which invites accidents". These points were considered in *Fraser v B N Furman (Productions)* (1967) and *W J Lane v Spratt* (1970).

In the former case Diplock LJ said that there were three issues to consider when interpreting the "reasonable care" condition, which in this case was worded in almost identical terms to that which is contained in the policy under consideration. Firstly, was it the insured (whether company or individual) who must take reasonable precautions; secondly, what was the extent of the obligation to take steps to prevent accidents and, thirdly, what was meant by reasonable? This was an employers' liability case in which the insured had been held liable for injuries suffered by its employee because of its failure to properly guard a piece of machinery.

In the litigation between the employer and employee the judge had stated that the machine in question was of the type which should have been guarded and was not, but that the employer probably never realised the sort of risk to which it was subjecting its employees. Nevertheless the failure to guard did amount to failure on the part of the employer to take proper care for the safety of its employees, thus subjecting them to quite unnecessary risk.

In the litigation between the employer and insurer Diplock LJ stated that it was necessary to consider what was reasonable between insured and insurer and not insured and employee. This comment makes it clear that, if the insured have been found to be negligent or in breach of statutory duty which requires reasonable care to be taken, the courts would not automatically find that there had been a lack of reasonable care in the context of the insurance contract. To do so would be inconsistent with the purpose of the policy as stated forcefully by Goddard LJ in *Woolfall and Rimmer Limited v Moyle*.

Diplock LJ went on to say that "reasonable" in the policy meant that the insured should not:

(a) deliberately court a danger, the existence of which he or she recognised, by refraining from taking any measures to avert it, and,
(b) that he or she should not act in a reckless manner by, having recognised the danger, not caring whether or not it is averted.

For further consideration of what is meant by "the Insured" it is necessary to return to *Woolfall and Rimmer Limited v Moyle* and a more recent case *Duncan Logan (Contractors) v Royal Exchange Assurance Group* (1973). The liability policy indemnifies the insured but it is normally the actions of employees that give rise to claims and, in the case of large limited companies, there could be many levels of management between the shareholders and directors, and such employees. It would therefore be easier for an insurer to rely on the exclusion where the insured is a sole trader or a small company under the direct control of the principal shareholder. There is no reason why an insurer could not apply the condition where its insured is a large limited company but it would have to show that the failure to take reasonable care (as established in the cases referred to above) was the responsibility of a senior director(s). In the *Duncan Logan* case it was held that the insured's obligation to take reasonable precautions was not breached by the negligence of one of its employees and in *Woolfall's* case it was held that the insured had complied with the condition by delegating the task of providing suitable and safe equipment to a competent foreman.

Policy conditions

In contrast to this in *British Food Freezers Limited v Industrial Estates Management for Scotland* (1977) the insured was held to be in breach of the reasonable care condition. The insured was a firm of contractors and, even though it had delegated responsibility to a contractor manager, there was no evidence that he had ever been given instructions about fire precautions. It would appear that the contractor was well aware of the risks involved in the particular type of work being performed and that its failure to take precautions or to give instructions to its employee as to what precautions should be taken amounted to a failure to take reasonable care as contemplated by Diplock LJ in *Woolfall and Rimmer Limited v Moyle*.

Notice of material changes

> 7. If at any time or from time to time any change shall occur materially varying any of the facts existing at the date of the proposal the Insured shall within seven days give notice in writing to the Company and shall pay such additional premium as the Company may require.

As stated earlier, it is an implied condition of all contracts of insurance that material facts are disclosed when the insured proposes for insurance and again at renewal. The insured is however under no duty to notify changes in risk during the policy period and this condition is therefore written into the policy to protect insurers and to allow them to charge additional premium for any increased risk brought about by a change.

Breach of the condition will not invalidate the policy but, as mentioned in Chapter 2, if the change amounts to a change in the business as declared by the insured and as described in the policy schedule insurers are not obliged to deal with any claim arising out of the new business. Furthermore, insurers may also protect themselves by imposing certain warranties on the policy to restrict the type of risk to which they might be exposed. An example of this would be a warranty on a building contractor's policy to the effect that the insured carries out no work involving tunnelling or excavations at a depth in excess of, say, three metres.

Notice of cancellation and adjustment of premiums

> 8. This Policy may be cancelled at any time by thirty days' notice by registered letter from the Company to the Insured's last known address and in such event the Company will return a pro rata portion of the premium (after adjustment in accordance with Condition 9 if necessary) for the unexpired part of the Period of Insurance.

9. If the premium for this Policy has been calculated on any estimates furnished by the Insured the Insured shall keep an accurate record containing all particulars relative thereto and shall at all times allow the Company to inspect such records. The Insured shall within one month of the expiry of each Period of Insurance furnish to the Company such particulars and information as the Company may require. The premium for such period shall thereupon be adjusted and the difference paid by or allowed to the Insured as the case may be subject however to any minimum premium hereon.

It is convenient to examine these two conditions together as they both make reference to the premium which is the consideration paid by the insured, as one party to the contract, to the insurer as the other party, in return for which the insurer agrees to provide an indemnity. Insurers very rarely exercise their rights under Condition 8 but may do so if, for example, they find that the insured is consistently unco-operative by not allowing them to carry out proper enquiries into the circumstances of incidents leading to or having led to claims.

The premium charged is usually based on the insured's estimates of turnover or wages paid for the period of insurance ahead and for this reason it is convenient for the policy period to coincide with the insured's financial year. The information is provided in the form of an annual declaration and Condition 9 allows for return of premium if the earlier estimates were too high or payment of an extra premium if too low. It also gives the insurer the right to inspect the insured's records if it has reason to believe that incorrect information has been given.

Premium calculation

There is no standard method of rating public liability policies. It is normal to base the premium rate on wages where the insured carries out work away from the premises and on turnover for large risks and for product liability risks.

Premises which are open to the general public, such as cinemas, hotels and sports grounds are charged on a capacity basis where the rate is applied to the number of seats, rooms or maximum possible attendances.

A *per capita* basis is used for small retail shops, the rate being applied to the number of employees, and premiums for farms and estates are calculated by reference to the total acreage.

Where liability cover for personal liabilities is included as part of household and similar policies a nominal premium is charged.

Truth of statements

10. The due observance and fulfilment of the terms conditions and endorsements of this policy insofar as they relate to anything to be done or complied with by the Insured and the truth of the statements and answers in the said proposal shall be conditions precedent to any liability of the Company to make any payment under this Policy.

It is an implied condition of the insurance contract that the truth of statements and answers in the proposal is a condition precedent to liability under the policy and this condition, together with the declaration on the proposal form, emphasises this and the fact that the proposal is part of the contract.

Compliance with terms and conditions

The condition also attempts to make compliance with all terms and conditions of the policy a condition precedent to liability but it is doubtful if such a condition would be upheld if tested by the courts. It is difficult to see what this clause adds to the other conditions, whether express or implied, which could not be stated as part of those conditions if the insurer considers that there is any doubt about the intention of those conditions. Furthermore, some of the conditions referred to are in fact stipulations rather than conditions and, recalling the *contra proferentem* rule, any ambiguity caused by Condition 10 would be construed against the insurer.

CHAPTER 9

Extensions to basic policy cover

The public liability policy, an example of which appears in Appendix A, can be extended or amended to meet the specific requirements of insured or insurer and the most common extensions, other than those which have already been examined, will be considered in this chapter. Some of these extensions are now included as part of certain insurers' "standard" policies, but where they are not it is normal for them to be incorporated by means of endorsement as and when required.

Joint insured clause

Many businesses, particularly large corporations and holding companies, comprise a number of individual companies with their own legal identities, and, rather than each company having a separate policy, it is more convenient for them all to be covered under one policy. This can be achieved by means of the joint insured clause but it is still preferable for all the individual companies to be identified by name on the policy and the expression "associated and/or subsidiary companies" is best avoided unless the companies are also specified. It is unlikely that this expression takes account of all companies which the insured may wish to include, such as those which are not subsidiaries but in which it has a controlling interest, and "associated" has no legal meaning in this context. By using the word "associated" insurers could find themselves indemnifying companies in whom the insured had no direct financial interest, such as regular customers or suppliers.

If other companies are covered by the policy it is important that full descriptions of their businesses are given and included under the heading "Description of Business" as otherwise the policy would only give cover for the business of the controlling or holding company, which might be quite different.

Cross liabilities clause

The "standard" policy excludes liability in respect of loss or damage to the insured's own property or to property in its custody or control. Therefore it would not be possible for one company to obtain an indemnity under the policy in respect of a liability incurred to another company in the same group if those two companies were insured under the same policy by virtue of a joint insured clause. This can be rectified, if the insured so requires, by means of a cross liabilities clause, thus allowing the company against which the claim is made to obtain the benefit of the policy.

The policy only provides a single limit of indemnity for the insured and all joint named insured's rather than a separate limit for each individual company. In other words the limit of indemnity is not increased by a factor equal to the total number of companies named.

Indemnity to directors, executives and employees

The policy indemnifies the insured alone. In many cases this will be a limited company with its own legal identity and the policy dces not therefore indemnify directors, executives or employees who may be sued in their own names either separately or jointly with the insured. Most insurers are willing to give the necessary cover either as part of their standard policy or by any endorsement which may be worded as follows:

> If any claim is made upon any director, executive or employee of the Insured and the claim is such that if made upon the Insured the Insured would be entitled to indemnity under this Policy the Company will at the request of the Insured and subject to the terms and limitations of this Policy indemnify the said director, executive or employee of the Insured in respect of such claim.
> Provided that;
> (a) such director, executive or employee is not entitled to indemnity under any other policy or policies
> (b) the extension by this Endorsement shall not apply to or include liability in respect of injury to any person under a contract of service or apprenticeship with the director, executive or employee where the injury arises out of and in the course of such person's employment or services with the director, executive or employee
> (c) such director, executive or employee shall as though he were the Insured observe fulfil and be subject to the terms exceptions limits and conditions of this Policy so far as they can apply
> (d) the extension by this Endorsement shall not operate to increase the Company's liability as set forth in the Schedule under the heading of Limit of

Indemnity beyond the amount or amounts for which the Company would be liable if the policy were not so extended.

It is not immediately evident why this clause would be necessary as the basic policy provides cover in respect of liabilities incurred by all employees when acting in the course of their employment and the manner in which the clause is worded makes it clear that no greater indemnity is given to employees than would be available to the insured. There is therefore no indemnity given to directors, executives or employees for liability incurred outside the course of their employment. It is possible, however, that they could be sued as private individuals in respect of actions committed during their employment and this clause makes it clear that they will be indemnified even if not named as an insured under the policy.

Inclusion of property in the insured's custody or control

The policy exception relating to property in the custody or control of the insured needs to be modified in certain cases as mentioned in the section dealing with that exception. Thus policies issued to hotels should cover liability in respect of guest's effects and goods left in cloakrooms, and contractors require cover for premises and their contents upon which they are temporarily performing work.

Tenant's legal liability

A tenant may incur liabilities for damage to property which he or she occupies either contractually, under the terms of a lease, or through negligence. Indemnity for such liability is excluded by the custody or control exception but, where the cover is required, the basic policy may be endorsed as follows:

> Property in the custody or control of the Insured shall not be deemed to include premises (including fixtures and fittings) leased or rented to the Insured, provided always that:
> (a) the premises are specified in the Schedule;
> (b) liability assumed by the Insured under agreement is excluded unless such liability would have attached notwithstanding such agreement.

The cover provided by this endorsement would probably be subject to an excess of at least £100 so that insurers would not have to deal with claims for minor damage to the tenanted property.

If the tenancy imposes contractual liability on the insured for certain types of damage (usually fire and water perils) this can usually be covered by a material damage policy which, if possible, should be arranged in the joint names of the landlord and the tenant. This would prevent the tenant or his or her insurers from exercising their right of recovery against the tenant in the event that damage was caused as a result of the tenant's negligence (*Petrofina (UK) Ltd v Magnaload Ltd* (1983)).

There is authority, however, that no right of recovery exists even if the tenant is not a joint insured under the relevant material damage policy. In *Mark Rowlands Ltd v Berni Inns Ltd* (1985) the Court of Appeal held that, although Berni Inns Ltd (the tenants) were not named on a policy covering the buildings a subrogation action by the insurers of Mark Rowlands Ltd (the landlords) would fail. Berni Inns Ltd were required to pay, as part of their rent, money equivalent to the premiums paid by the landlord for insuring the premises against fire and this was one of the principal factors in the Court of Appeal decision.

Sports, social and welfare organisations

If these facilities are provided by the insured the policy can be extended to cover the committees of such organisations in the same way as the directors, executives and employees clause.

Private work for directors or senior executives

It is not unusual for directors or senior executives to ask employees to carry out private work such as repairs at their homes. The policy can be extended to indemnify the insured and the directors and senior executives in respect of injury loss or damage to third parties.

Territorial limits

As already mentioned the policy does give certain limited cover for employees working outside the territorial limits. If cover is required for overseas contracts insurers are generally reluctant to allow any extension

Extensions to basic policy cover

if this is likely to expose them to litigation in countries outside the territorial limits. Such litigation would be likely in any territory where the insured has permanent offices or other representation which could be the object of legal proceedings. Therefore, if insurers do extend the policy to cover overseas work outside the territorial limits this would exclude legal actions in any such countries or territories.

This is a particularly serious problem in the USA where the principle of strict liability applies to many areas of tort law and awards for damages are very high due to the fact that they are made by juries and that plaintiffs' lawyers are paid on a contingency fee basis whereby they make no charge if the claim is lost but take a percentage of the damages if the claim is won.

APPENDIX A

Public liability policy

Whereas the Insured carrying on the Business described in the Schedule and no other for the purpose of this insurance by a proposal and declaration which shall be the basis of this contract and be deemed to be incorporated herein has applied to the Company for the insurance hereinafter contained and has paid or agreed to pay the premium as consideration for or on account of such insurance.

Now this policy witnesseth that the company will subject to the terms exceptions limits and conditions contained herein or endorsed hereon indemnify the Insured against all sums which the Insured shall become legally liable to pay as damages in respect of:

1. Accidental bodily injury to any person;
2. Accidental loss of or damage to property;

happening in connection with the Business and occurring within the Territorial Limits during the Period of Insurance.

Provided that the Liability of the Company for all damages payable to any claimant or any number of claimants in respect of or arising out of any one occurrence or in respect of or arising out of all occurrences of a series consequent on or attributable to one source or original cause shall not exceed the Limit of Indemnity specified in the Schedule for any one Period of Insurance.

In respect of a claim for damages to which the indemnity expressed in the policy applies the Company will also indemnify the Insured against:

(a) all costs and expenses of litigation recovered by any claimant from the Insured;
(b) all costs and expenses of litigation incurred with the written consent of the Company;

(c) the solicitor's fee for representation at any coroner's or fatal enquiry or in any court of summary jurisdiction.

In the event of the death of the Insured the Company will in respect of the liability incurred by the Insured indemnify the Insured's personal representatives in the terms of and subject to the limitations of this Policy provided that such personal representatives shall as though they were the Insured observe fulfil and be subject to the terms exceptions and conditions of the policy so far as they can apply.

Exceptions

The policy does not cover:

1. Liability in respect of injury to any person under a contract of service or apprenticeship with the Insured where such injury arises out of and in the course of such person's employment or service with the Insured.

2. Liability in respect of loss or damage to property:
   (a) belonging to the Insured
   (b) in the charge or under the control of the Insured but this exception shall not apply to property belonging to any servant of the Insured.
   (c) caused by or through or in connection with the bursting of any economiser used in conjunction with a steam boiler or any boiler vessel or other apparatus which is intended to operate under internal pressure due to steam and belonging to or in the charge or under the control of the Insured.

3. Liability in respect of injury loss or damage caused by or through or in connection with:
   (a) Any passenger lift passenger elevator or passenger escalator owned by or in the possession of the Insured. This Exception shall not apply in respect of the occasional carriage of passengers on any goods lift goods elevator or goods escalator.
   (b) The ownership or possession or use by or on behalf of the Insured of:
   (i) any vehicle (or machine) which is capable of self-propulsion or attached to a self-propelled vehicle and used in circumstances to which the Road Traffic Acts apply; or
   (ii) any vehicle (or machine) which is insured for the benefit of the Insured under any form of Motor Insurance Policy; or

(iii) any vessel or craft not specified in the Schedule under the heading of Plant.
(c) Remedial or professional or other advice or treatment (other than medical first aid treatment) given or administered or omitted by the Insured.
(d) Any goods or any container thereof sold or supplied or repaired or renovated or let on hire or handled by the Insured and no longer in the Insured's custody or control.
(e) The ownership or tenure by the Insured of any land or building not specified in the Schedule under the heading of The Premises.

4. Liability assumed by the Insured by agreement unless such liability would have attached to the Insured notwithstanding such agreement.

5. Any legal liability of whatsoever nature directly or indirectly caused by or contributed to by or arising from ionising radiations or contamination by radioactivity from any nuclear fuel or from any nuclear waste from the combustion of nuclear fuel.

6. Liability for any consequence of war invasion act of foreign enemy hostilities (whether war be declared or not) civil war rebellion revolution insurrection or military or usurped power.

In these Exceptions the expression "vessel or craft" shall include any vessel craft or thing made or intended to float on or in or travel on or through water or air.

Conditions

This Policy and the Schedule shall be read together as one contract and any word or expression to which a specific meaning has been attached in any part of this Policy or of the Schedule shall bear such specific meaning wherever it may appear.

1. The Insured shall give written notice to the Head Office or Branch Office of the Company of any injury loss or damage or claim or proceedings immediately the same shall have come to the knowledge of the Insured or his representative.

2. The Insured shall not without the consent in writing of the Company repudiate liability negotiate or make any admission offer promise or payment in connection with any injury loss or damage or claim and the

Company shall be entitled if it so desires to take over and conduct in the name of the Insured the defence of any claim or to prosecute in the name of the Insured at its own expense and for its own benefit any claim for indemnity or damages or otherwise against any persons and shall have full discretion in the conduct of any proceedings and in the settlement of any claim and the Insured shall give all such information and assistance as the Company may require.

3. The Company may in the case of any injury loss or damage pay to the Insured the Limit of Indemnity for any one accident (but deducting therefrom in such case any sum or sums already paid as damages in respect thereof) or any lesser sum for which the claim or claims arising therefrom can be settled and the Company shall thereafter be under no further liability in respect of such injury loss or damage except for the payment of costs and expenses of litigation referred to on the first page of this Policy and specified in items (a) and (b) thereof incurred prior to the date of the payment of such Limit of Indemnity or such lesser sum.

4. If at the time of any claim arising under this insurance there shall be any other insurance covering the same risk or part thereof the Company shall not be liable for more than its rateable proportion thereof.

5. The Company may at all reasonable times for the purpose of enquiry or examination by their authorised officials and agents enter into any premises or places to which this insurance applies or in which injury loss or damage has occurred and may remain in possession for a reasonable period for the purpose of such enquiry or examination and the Insured shall give all necessary facilities in connection therewith.

6. The Insured shall exercise reasonable care in the selection of competent employees and shall take all reasonable precautions to prevent injury loss or damage.

7. If at any time or from time to time any change shall occur materially varying any of the facts existing at the date of the proposal the Insured shall within seven days give notice in writing to the Company and shall pay such additional premium as the Company may require.

8. This Policy may be cancelled at any time by thirty days' notice by registered letter from the Company to the Insured's last known address and in such event the Company will return a pro rata portion of the premium (after adjustment in accordance with Condition 9 if necessary) for the unexpired part of the Period of Insurance.

9. If the premium for this Policy has been calculated on any estimates furnished by the Insured the Insured shall keep an accurate record containing all particulars relative thereto and shall at all times allow the Company to inspect such records. The Insured shall within one month of the expiry of each Period of Insurance furnish to the Company such particulars and information as the Company may require. The premium for such period shall thereupon be adjusted and the difference paid by or allowed to the Insured as the case may be subject however to any minimum premium hereon.

10. The due observance and fulfilment of the terms conditions and endorsements of this Policy insofar as they relate to anything to be done or complied with by the Insured and the truth of the statements and answers in the said proposal shall be conditions precedent to any liability of the Company to make any payment under this Policy.

The Schedule

The Insured:	Name Address
The Business:	
The Premises:	
Plant:	
Period of Insurance:	1. From the _____ to the _____ (both dates inclusive) 2. Any subsequent annual period for which the Insured shall pay and the Company shall agree to accept a renewal premium.
Premiums:	£_____ £_____ £_____ First Renewal Minimum
Limit of Indemnity:	£_____
Injury:	"Bodily injury to any person" shall mean death or illness of or bodily injury to any person.
The Territorial Limits:	Great Britain the Republic of Ireland Northern Ireland the Channel Islands or the Isle Man but in respect of business journeys and the like (excluding the supervision or execution of any work or contract) anywhere in the World.
Signature	Signed this ____ day of _____ 19 ____ Checked.

APPENDIX B

Sun Alliance Insurance Group liability insurance proposal

SUN ALLIANCE
LIABILITY INSURANCE

Proposal

(For trades in the building or construction industry, please see separate Proposal)

All insurances are underwritten for the Group by Sun Alliance and London Insurance plc (incorporated in England).

Please return this form to:–

Please use block letters and tick boxes where approrpiate. Where requested, please enter further details in space provided.

Name of Proposer in full

Tel. No.

Address

	Postcode

Address of all your business premises | Description eg office, factory

A. YOUR BUSINESS

1 Full description of your activities

2 Date established [ ]

3 Will you undertake any manual work from your premises?
(other than delivery)   Yes ☐   No ☐

If "Yes", state nature of this work and total estimated wages applicable for next 12 months. Please also answer questions a) to d)

	£

Will any of this work
a) be outside the UK?   Yes ☐   No ☐

If "Yes", give details and estimated wages applicable for next 12 months

	£

b) be offshore? Yes ☐ No ☐

If "Yes", state nature of work and estimated wages applicable for next 12 months

	£

c) involve the use of welding, flame cutting equipment, blowlamps or hot air paint strippers? Yes ☐ No ☐

If "Yes", state nature of work and estimated wages applicable for next 12 months

	£

d) be sub-contracted to

    i) established firms? Yes ☐ No ☐
    ii) others? (including self-employed persons) Yes ☐ No ☐

If "Yes", give details and estimated payments applicable for next 12 months

i)	£
ii)	£

4 Will you supply any products? Yes ☐ No ☐
If "Yes", give details, including purpose of use and estimated turnover applicable for next 12 months for each

Please also supply specimen brochures and answer questions a) to e)

	£
	£
	£

a) Will you supply any products that you do not manufacture? Yes ☐ No ☐

If "Yes",

    i) Do you retain rights of recovery against the manufacturers? Yes ☐ No ☐

    ii) Do you alter, adapt or change the form of any product which you do not manufacture? Yes ☐ No ☐

If "Yes", give details, including the product involved, purpose of use, nature of supplier and type of alteration, adaption or change made

iii) Give details of imported products including purpose of use, source and estimated turnover applicable for next 12 months for each

	£
	£

b) Will any of your products be used
i) in aircraft? Yes ☐ No ☐

ii) offshore? Yes ☐ No ☐

If "Yes", state purpose of use and estimated turnover applicable for next 12 months for each

i)	£
ii)	£

c) What are the major hazards associated with the products you supply?

Have you warned users of these hazards? Yes ☐ No ☐

If "Yes", please supply samples of any brochures, labels, leaflets or instructions.

d) Will you design, give advice on or prepare specifications for any products you supply? Yes ☐ No ☐

If "Yes", please give details, including products involved and design staff qualifications and experience

> **Note** You should supply relevant extracts from your design manual if available

e) Will any system of check be in operation to discover possible defects in products?   Yes ☐   No ☐

If "Yes", give details of procedure

f) Will any of your products be supplied directly, or to your knowledge indirectly, to the USA or Canada?   Yes ☐   No ☐

If "Yes", please state

i) Details and purpose of use

ii) Estimated turnover applicable to products to be supplied to the USA and Canada for next 12 months

USA	£
Canada	£

5 Have any of your products previously been supplied directly, or to your knowledge indirectly, to the USA or Canada?   Yes ☐   No ☐

If "Yes", give details, including purpose of use and turnover applicable to each of the last 3 years

	USA	Canada
19	£	£
19	£	£
19	£	£

6 Have you any representation outside the UK?   Yes ☐   No ☐

If "Yes", state nature and territories involved

7 Do you have any contracts or agreements with any customers, suppliers or sellers? Yes ☐ No ☐

If "Yes", please supply copies

8 Will you provide any service or treatment other than the supply of products? Yes ☐ No ☐

If "Yes", give details and estimated turnover applicable for next 12 months

	£
	£
	£

9 Will you, or your employees, handle or come into contact with any industrial dust (eg asbestos, silica or cotton), radioactive materials, or any other substance or conditions which may be harmful to health? Yes ☐ No ☐

If "Yes", give details and state safety procedures applying

Sun Alliance Insurance Group liability insurance proposal

B. WAGES AND TURNOVER

1 Please complete as necessary

Description of all employees. Wages, but not fees, of working directors should be included	Estimated Number	Estimated wages and salaries for next 12 months	
		At your premises	Away from your premises
Clerical (not engaged in manual work)		£	£
All Others (specify below):		£ £ £ £ £	£ £ £ £ £

2 Total estimated wages and salaries for next 12 months £ _____

3 Total estimated turnover for next 12 months £ _____

C. GENERAL QUESTIONS

The following questions must be answered in all cases

1 Have you been prosecuted during the last 5 years under any safety legislation? Yes ☐ No ☐

If "Yes", give full details, including date and outcome

2 Has any insurer ever declined to insure you or refused to renew or terminated any of your insurances? Yes ☐ No ☐

If "Yes", give details, including reason and name of insurer

3 Give name(s) of present liability insurer(s) and expiry date(s) of cover

4 Have you or any of your directors or partners ever been convicted of or charged with (but not yet tried for) a criminal offence other than a motoring offence?   Yes ☐   No ☐

If "Yes", give details

5 Give details of any business in which you or any of your directors or partners are or have been involved during the last 5 years

Name of Business	Trade	From	To

6 Have you become aware during the last 5 years of any injury to or death disease or illness arising out of your business of

    a) employees?   Yes ☐   No ☐

    b) members of the public or damage to their property?   Yes ☐   No ☐

If "Yes", in either case please give details

Brief Circumstances – including date (whether claim made or not)	Amount paid £	Amount Outstanding £
a)		
b)		

D. YOUR REQUIREMENTS

1 Do you require

    a) Employers' Liability? Yes ☐ No ☐

    b) Public/Products Liability? Yes ☐ No ☐

    If "Yes", state limit of indemnity required **(recommended minimum £1,000,000)** £ _____

    c) Quotations for alternative limits? Yes ☐ No ☐

    If "Yes", please state alternative limits
    £ _____
    £ _____
    £ _____

    d) Additional Cover? Yes ☐ No ☐

    If "Yes", please give details

2 Do you wish to pay the premium by monthly instalments? Yes ☐ No ☐

3 Date from which cover is to commence

Declaration
I/We declare that to the best of my/our knowledge and belief the above statements are true and complete and will form part of the contract between me/us and the Company.

Signature [   ]   Date [   ]

(signing this form does not bind you to complete the insurance)

We recommend that you should keep a record, including copies of letters and this proposal form, of all information supplied to us for the purpose of entering into this insurance contract.

Please let us know if you would like a copy of this proposal from sent to you.

Reproduced by permission of the Sun Alliance Insurance Group.

APPENDIX C

Sun Alliance Insurance Group liability policy

PLEASE READ THIS POLICY (AND THE SCHEDULE WHICH FORMS AN INTEGRAL PART OF THE POLICY) TO ENSURE THAT IT MEETS YOUR REQUIREMENTS

Sun Alliance and London Insurance plc (incorporated in England and herein called the Company) and the Insured agree that

The Policy the Schedule (including any Schedule issued in substitution) and any Memoranda shall be considered one document and any word or expression to which a specific meaning has been attached shall bear such meaning wherever it appears

The Proposal or any information supplied by the Insured shall be incorporated in the contract

The Company will provide the insurance described in this Policy subject to the terms and conditions for the Period of Insurance shown in the Schedule and any subsequent period for which the insured shall pay and the Company shall agree to accept the premium

Provided that this Policy shall not be in force unless it has been initialled by an authorised official of the Company

Chief General Manager

Initialled

General Conditions

1 Observance of the terms of this Policy relating to anything to be done or complied with by the Insured or any other party entitled to indemnity is a condition precedent to any liability of the Company except in so far as is necessary to comply with the requirements of any legislation enacted in Great Britain Northern Ireland the Channel Islands or the Isle of Man relating to compulsory insurance of legal liability to employees.

2 The Insured at his own expense shall
   A) take reasonable precautions to
      1) prevent damage to the property insured
      2) prevent any occurrence
      3) cease any activity
   which may give rise to liability under this Policy
   B) maintain all buildings furnishings ways works machinery plant and vehicles in sound condition
   C) as soon as possible after discovery clause any defect or danger to be made good or remedied and in the meantime shall cause such additional precautions to be taken as the circumstances may require

3 If any part of the premium is based on estimates provided by the Insured the Insured shall keep an accurate record containing all relevant particulars and shall allow the Company to inspect such record The Insured shall within one month after the expiry of each Period of Insurance provide such information as the Company may require The premium shall then be adjusted and the difference paid by or allowed to the Insured subject to any minimum premium the Company may have imposed

4 If at any time of any claim there is or but for the existence of this Policy would be any other insurance covering the same loss destruction or damage or legal liability the Company shall not be liable under this Policy to indemnify the Insured except in respect of any amount beyond that which would have been payable under such insurance had this Policy not been effected.

Sun Alliance Insurance Group liability policy

Schedule No.   Policy No.

Branch

Agency No.

Insured

Business

Period of Insurance

From

To   Renewal Date

Premium £   Renewal Premium £

Section 1 **Employer's Liability**

                                                                 Limit of Indemnity

Section 2 **Public/Products Liability**

          A) Any one Event   £

          B) All Events happening
             during any Period of
             Insurance in respect of
             products supplied   £

Date

Liability Insurance

The Company will indemnify

1 the Insured

2 the personal representatives of the Insured in respect of legal liability incurred by the Insured

3 at the request of the Insured
   - A) any principal
   - B) any director of the Insured
   - C) any Person Employed

   against legal liability in respect of which the Insured would have been entitled to indemnity under this Policy if the claim had been made against the Insured
   - D) the officers committees and members of the Insured's canteen social sports and welfare organisations and first aid fire and ambulance services in their respective capacities as such
   - E) any director or partner of the Insured or Employee in respect of private work undertaken by any Person Employed for such director partner or Employee with the prior consent of the Insured

each of whom shall as though the Insured be subject to the terms of this Policy so far as they can apply

For the purposes of Liability Insurance
- A) Person Employed means any
  1) Employee meaning person under a contract of service or apprenticeship with the Insured
  2) labour master and persons supplied by him
  3) person employed by labour only sub-contractors
  4) self-employed person
  5) person hired to or borrowed by the Insured
  6) person undertaking study or work experience
- B) the Business is conducted at or from premises in Great Britain Northern Ireland the Channel Islands or the Isle of Man and shall include
  1) ownership repair and maintenance of the Insured's own property
  2) provision and management of canteen social sports and welfare organisations for the benefit of any Person Employed and first aid fire and ambulance services
  3) private work undertaken by any Person Employed for any director or partner of the Insured or Employee with the prior consent of the Insured

Section 1 Employers' Liability

The Company will provide indemnity
1 against legal liability for damages and claimant's costs and expenses in respect of bodily injury to or death disease or illness of any Person Employed caused during any Period of Insurance

    A) in Great Britain Northern Ireland the Channel Islands or the Isle of Man

or

    B) while temporarily outside these territories

arising out of and in the course of employment by the Insured in the Business

2 in respect of

    A) costs of legal representation at

        1) any coroner's inquest or inquiry in respect of any death
        2) proceedings in any court arising out of any alleged breach of statutory duty resulting in bodily injury death disease or illness

    which may be the subject of indemnity under this Section

    B) all other costs and expenses in relation to any matter which may form the subject of a claim for indemnity under **1** above

incurred with the Company's written consent

Exclusion to Section 1

The indemnity will not apply to any legal liability of whatsoever nature directly or indirectly caused by or contributed to by or arising from

    A) ionising radiations or contamination by radioactivity from any nuclear fuel or from any nuclear waste from the combustion of nuclear fuel
    B) the radioactive toxic explosive or other hazardous properties of any explosive nuclear assembly or nuclear component thereof

where such legal liability is

    1) that of any principal
    2) accepted under agreement and would not have attached in the absence of such agreement

Extension to Section 1 (each of which is subject otherwise to the terms of this Policy)

1 Unsatisfied Court Judgements

In the event of a judgement for damages being obtained

A) by any Employee of the personal representatives of any Employee in respect of bodily injury to or death disease or illness of the Employee caused during any Period of Insurance and arising out of and in the course of employment by the Insured in the Business

B) against any company or individual operating from premises within Great Britain Northern Ireland the Channel Islands or the Isle of Man

in any court situated in the territories specified in B) above and

C) remaining unsatisfied in whole or in part six months after the date of such judgement

the Company will pay to the Employee or the personal representatives of the Employee at the request of the Insured the amount of any such damages and any awarded costs to the extent that they remain unsatisfied

Provided that

A) there is no appeal outstanding

B) if any payment is made under the terms of this Extension the Employee or the personal representatives of the Employee shall assign the judgement to the Company

2 Compensation for Court Attendance

In the event of any of the undermentioned persons attending court as a witness at the request of the Company in connection with a claim in respect of which the Insured is entitled to indemnity under Section 1 the Company will provide compensation to the Insured at the following rates per day for each day on which attendance is required

A) any director or partner of the Insured   £250
B) any Employee   £100

3 Health and Safety at Work – Legal Defence Costs

The Company will provide indemnity to the Insured and if the Insured so requests any director or partner of the Insured or Person Employed in respect of

A) legal costs and other expenses incurred with the Company's written consent
B) costs awarded against the Insured or any director partner or Person Employed

in connection with the defence of any criminal proceedings brought or in appeal against conviction arising from such proceedings in respect of a breach of the Health and Safety at Work Act 1974 or the Health and Safety at Work (Northern Ireland) Order 1978

Provided that

A) the proceedings relate to

1) the health safety and welfare of any Person Employed
and
2) an offence alleged to have been committed during the Period of Insurance and in the course of the Insured's Business

B) the indemnity will not apply

1) to fines or penalties of any kind
2) where indemnity is provided by any other insurance
3) to proceedings consequent upon any deliberate act or omission

Section 2 Public/Products Liability

The Company will provide indemnity
1 up to the Limit of Indemnity against legal liability for damages in respect of accidental

   A) Injury (meaning bodily injury to or death disease illness wrongful arrest invasion of the right of privacy detention wrongful imprisonment or wrongful eviction of any person)
   B) loss of or damage to material property
   C) nuisance trespass or interference with any easement right of air light water or way

   happening during any Period of Insurance in connection with the Business

2 against legal liability for claimant's costs and expenses in connection with 1 above

3 in respect of

   A) costs of legal representation at

   1) any coroner's inquest or inquiry in respect of any death
   2) proceedings in any court arising out of any alleged breach of statutory duty resulting in any occurrence specified in 1 above

   which may be the subject of indemnity under this Section

   B) all other costs and expenses in relation to any matter which may form the subject of a claim for indemnity under 1 above

incurred with the Company's written consent

Provided that in respect of any one Event (meaning one occurrence or all occurrences of a series consequent on or attributable to one source or original cause) or all Events happening during any Period of Insurance in respect of products supplied
1 the Insured's Contribution (meaning the amount or amounts specified in the Schedule which the Insured agrees to pay) in respect of damages and claimant's costs and expenses will be payable before the Company shall be liable to make any payment
2 the Company may at any time pay the Limit of Indemnity (less any sums already paid as damages) or any less amount for which the claims arising out of such Event can be settled The Company will then

relinquish control of such claims and be under no further liability in rspect thereof except for costs and expenses for which the Company may be responsible in respect of matters prior to the date of such payment

3 where the Company is liable to indemnify more than one party the total amount of indemnity in respect of damages shall not exceed the Limit of Indemnity

Exclusions to Section 2

The indemnity will not apply to legal liability

1 arising out of the ownership possession or use by or on behalf of the Insured or any person entitled to indemnity of any
   A) mechanically propelled vehicle other than legal liability arising out of
      1) the use of plant as a tool of trade on site
      2) the use of plant at the premises of the Insured
      3) the loading or unloading of any vehicle
      except where indemnity is provided by any motor insurance contract or where insurance or security is required by law
   B) aircraft or other aerial device
   C) aerospatial device
   D) hovercraft
   E) water-borne craft (other than hand-propelled or sailing craft in inland or territorial waters)

2 for bodily injury to or death disease or illness of any Person Employed arising out of and in the course of employment by the Insured in the Business

3 in respect of loss or damage to any property which at the time of the Event giving rise to such legal liability is owned by or held in trust by or in the custody or control of the Insured other than
   A) Employees' directors' partners' or visitors' personal effects including vehicles and their contents
   B) premises and their contents not owned by or leased or rented to the insured at which the Insured is undertaking work in connection with the Business
   C) premises and their fixtures and fittings leased or rented to the Insured unless such legal liability arises from and agreement to maintain in force insurance in respect of loss of or damage to such premises and their fixtures and fittings

4 A) in respect of loss of or damage to any
      1) product supplied
      2) contract work executed   } by the Insured
   caused by any defect therein or the unsuitability thereof for its intended purpose
   B) for the costs of recall removal repair alteration replacement or reinstatement of any
      1) product supplied
      2) contract work executed   } by the Insured
   necessitated by any defect therein or the unsuitability thereof for its intended purpose

5 arising out or in connection with any
      A) product supplied
      B) contract work executed   } by the Insured
   where such legal liability has been accepted by agreement unless such liability would have attached in the absence of such agreement

6 arising out of or in connection with
      A) advice
      B) design   } provided for a fee
      C) specification

7 for the cost of remedying any defect or alleged defect in premises disposed of by the Insured

8 of whatsoever nature directly or indirectly caused by or contributed to by or arising from
   A) ionising radiations or contamination by radioactivity from any nuclear fuel or from any nuclear waste from the combustion of nuclear fuel
   B) the radioactive toxic explosive or other hazardous properties of any explosive nuclear assembly or nuclear component thereof

9 arising from any consequence of war invasion act of foreign enemy hostilities (whether war be declared or not) civil war rebellion revolution insurrection of military or usurped power

Extensions to Section 2 (each of which is subject otherwise to the terms of this Policy)

1 Cross Liabilities

If the Insured comprises more than one party the Company will provide

Sun Alliance Insurance Group liability policy

indemnity to each in the same manner and to the same extent as if a separate Policy had been issued to each

Provided that the total amount payable in respect of damages shall not exceed the Limit of Indemnity

2 Compensation for Court Attendance

In the event of any of the undermentioned persons attending court as a witness at the request of the Company in connection with a claim in respect of which the Insured is entitled to indemnity under Section 2 the Company will provide compensation to the Insured at the following rates per day for each day on which attendance is required

A) any director or partner of the Insured   £250
B) any Employee   £100

3 Contingent Motor Liability

Notwithstanding Exclusion 1A) the Company will provide indemnity to the Insured against legal liability arising out of the use in the course of the Business of any motor vehicle not the property of nor provided by the Insured

The indemnity will not apply to legal liability

A) in respect of loss of or damage to such vehicle or to property conveyed therein
B) arising while such vehicle is being driven by the Insured
C) in respect of which the Insured is entitled to indemnity under any other insurance
D) arising outside Great Britain Northern Ireland and Channel Islands or the Isle of Man

4 Health and Safety at Work – Legal Defence Costs

The Company will provide indemnity to the Insured and if the Insured so requests any director or partner of the Insured or Person Employed in respect of

A) legal costs and other expenses incurred with the Company's written consent
B) costs awarded against the Insured or any director partner or Person Employed

in connection with the defence of any criminal proceedings brought or in appeal against conviction arising from such proceedings in respect of a breach of the Health and Safety at Work Act 1974 or the Health and Safety at Work (Northern Ireland) Order 1978

Provided that

A) the proceedings relate to

1) the health safety and welfare of any person other than a Person Employed
and
2) an offence alleged to have been committed during the Period of Insurance and in the course of the Insured's Business

B) the indemnity will not apply

1) to fines or penalties of any kind
2) where indemnity is provided by any other insurance
3) to proceedings consequent upon any deliberate act or omission

5 Consumer Protection Act – Legal Defence Costs

The Company will provide indemnity to the Insured and if the Insured so requests any director or partner of the Insured or Person Employed in respect of

A) legal costs and other expenses incurred with the Company's written consent
B) costs awarded against the Insured or any director partner or Person Employed

in connection with the defence of any criminal proceedings brought or in appeal against conviction arising from such proceedings in respect of a breach of Part II of the Consumer Protection Act 1987

Provided that

A) the proceedings relate to an offence alleged to have been committed during the Period of Insurance and in the course of the Insured's Business

B) the indemnity will not apply

1) to fines or penalties of any kind
2) where indemnity is provided by any other insurance
3) to proceedings consequent upon any deliberate act or omission

6 Overseas Personal Liability

The Company will provide indemnity to the Insured and if the Insured so requests any director or partner of the Insured or Employee against legal liability incurred in a personal capacity while temporarily outside Great Britain Northern Ireland the Channel Islands or the Isle of Man in connection with the Business

The indemnity will not apply

A) to legal liability arising out of the ownership or occupation of land or buildings
B) where indemnity is provided by any other insurance

7 Data Protection Act 1984 – Reciprocal Sharing Agreement

In respect of the indemnity provided under Section 2 the Business shall include the provision of any reciprocal arrangement for the storage or processing of computer data or for use of computer facilities

Provided that the indemnity will not apply to legal liability in respect of any loss or damage sustained by any party to such an arrangement

Conditions applicable to Liability Insurance

The Insured shall give to the Company immediate written notice with full particulars of any occurrence which may give rise to a claim (regardless of the Insured's Contribution)

Every letter claim writ summons and process in connection with such occurrence shall be forwarded to the Company immediately on receipt

Written notice shall also be given by the Insured to the Company immediately the Insured shall have knowledge of any prosecution inquest or inquiry in connection with any occurrence which may give rise to liability under this Policy

No admission offer promise payment or indemnity shall be made or given by or on behalf of the Insured without the written consent of the Company which shall be entitled to take over and conduct in the name of the Insured the defence or settlement of any claim or to prosecute any claim in the name of the Insured for its own benefit and shall have full discretion in the conduct of any proceedings and in the settlement of any claim

The Insured shall give all such assistance as the Company may require

Reproduced by permission of the Sun Alliance Insurance Group.

APPENDIX D

Colonia Insurance Company (UK) Limited liability policy

SECTION 1 – PUBLIC LIABILITY

1. **INSURANCE COVER**

    1.1 **Indemnity**
    Indemnity against liability at law for damages and claimants costs and expenses in respect of

    1.1.1. accidental bodily injury (including death or disease) to any person and accidental loss of or damage to material property
    1.1.2. accidental trespass nuisance or interference with any easement of air light water or way

    occurring within the Territorial Limits during the Period of Insurance.

    1.2 **Defence Costs**
    The Company will pay all costs and expenses incurred with the written consent of the Company in the defence of settlement of any claim covered under Clause **1.1**.

    1.3 **Solicitors' Fees**
    The Company will also pay Solicitors' Fees.

2. **LIMIT OF INDEMNITY**

    The liability of the Company under this Section for all damages arising out of one occurrence or series of occurrences consequent on one original cause shall not exceed the Limit of Indemnity stated in the Schedule.

3. EXCEPTIONS TO SECTION 1

3.1 The Company will not indemnify the Insured against liability in respect of loss of or damage to property belonging to or held in trust by or in the custody or control of the Insured or of any Employee other than

    3.1.1. Employees' and visitors' clothing and personal effects (including vehicles and their contents)

    3.1.2. buildings (including contents) not owned or rented by the Insured but temporarily occupied for the purpose of work to such buildings provided that liability for the loss or damage arises otherwise than under the terms of a contract or agreement

    3.1.3. any premises leased hired or rented to the Insured to the extent that the Insured may be held liable otherwise than under any specific contract or agreement provided that the Company shall not be responsible for the first £250 of such loss or damage caused otherwise than by fire or explosion

3.2 The Company will not indemnify the Insured in respect of liability rising directly or indirectly by through or in connection with the ownership possession or use of

    3.2.1. any mechanically propelled vehicle whilst in use in circumstances in which a Certificate of Motor Insurance or surety is required

    3.2.2. any aircraft hovercraft drilling platform or rig or watercraft (except manually propelled watercraft)

3.3 The Company will not indemnify the Insured in respect of

    3.3.1. injury loss or damage arising out of any Products (after they have ceased to be in the custody or under the control of the Insured) other than food or drink for consumption on the Insured's premises

    3.3.2. the payment of penalties fines or liquidated damages

    3.3.3. the amount of the Excess shown in the Schedule

SECTION 2 – PRODUCTS LIABILITY

4. **INSURANCE COVER**

    4.1 Indemnity
    Indemnity against liability at law for damages and claimants costs and expenses in respect of bodily injury (including death or disease) to any person and loss of or damage to material property occurring within the Territorial Limits during the Period of Insurance and caused by any Products after they have ceased to be in the custody or under the control of the Insured.

    4.2 Defence Costs
    The Company will pay all costs and expenses incurred with the written consent of the Company in the defence or settlement of any claim covered under Clause 4.1.

    4.3 Solicitors' Fees
    The Company will also pay Solicitors' Fees

5. **LIMIT OF INDEMNITY**

    The liability of the Company under this Section for all damages in respect of bodily injury loss or damage occurring in any one Period of Insurance shall not in the aggregate exceed the Limit of Indemnity stated in the Schedule.

6. **EXCEPTIONS TO SECTION 2**

    The Company will not indemnify the Insured against liability in respect of

    6.1 loss of or damage to property belonging to or in the custody or control of the Insured or of an Employee

    6.2 injury loss or damage arising from food or drink for consumption on the Insured's premises

    6.3 injury loss or damage which is assumed by the Insured by agreement (other than liability arising out of condition or warranty of goods implied by law) unless such liability would have attached in the absence of such agreement

- **6.4** loss or damage to any Products or any costs or expenses incurred by anyone in repairing after replacing recalling or making any refund in respect of any Products.

- **6.5** injury loss or damage arising out of any Products which the Insured know or should reasonably know are intended for incorporation into the structure machinery or controls of any aircraft hovercraft or watercraft

- **6.6** injury loss or damage arising out of any Products which the Insured know or should reasonably know are to be delivered or used in the United States of America or Canada.

EXTENSIONS TO SECTIONS 1 AND/OR 2

7. HEALTH AND SAFETY AT WORK ETC. ACT 1974 DEFENCE COSTS

The Company will subject to the terms exceptions and conditions of this Policy indemnify the Insured in respect of

- **7.1** Legal costs and expenses incurred with the written consent of the Company

- **7.2** Legal costs and expenses awarded against the Insured or Director or Employee of the Insured

in connection with the defence of any prosecution (including an appeal against any conviction resulting from a prosecution) as a result of an alleged offence involving injury only to a person (or more than one) who is not an employee and occurring during the Period of Insurance under the Health and Safety at Work etc. Act 1974 or similar safety legislation of Great Britain, Northern Ireland the Channel Islands or The Isle of Man.

Provided always that the Company shall not be liable

- **7.3** for the payment of fines or penalties

- **7.4** where the prosecution results from a deliberate act or omission

8. CONTINGENT LIABILITY (NON-OWNED VEHICLES)

In respect of Section 1 only the Company will subject to the terms exceptions and conditions of this Policy indemnify the Insured named in the Schedule and no other person who might otherwise fall within the definition of Insured under Clause 15 for the purpose of this extension in respect of liability for bodily injury loss or damage to property arising out of the use of any motor vehicle (not the property of nor provided by the Insured) in connection with the Business provided always that the Company shall not be liable for

8.1 loss of or damage to any vehicle

8.2 injury loss of or damage resulting while such vehicle is being

    8.2.1. driven by the Insured

    8.2.2. driven with the general consent of the Insured or of his representative by any person who to the knowledge of the Insured or of such representative does not hold a licence to drive such vehicles unless such person has held and is not disqualified from holding or obtaining such a licence.

    8.2.3. used elsewhere than in Great Britain, Northern Ireland the Channel Islands or The Isle of Man

8.3 injury loss or damage for which the Insured is entitled to indemnity under any other insurance

9. DEFECTIVE PREMISES

The Company will subject to the terms exceptions and conditions of this Policy indemnify the Insured against liability in respect of bodily injury or loss of or damage to property arising in respect of any premises which have been disposed of by the Insured and which prior to such disposal were occupied by the Insured for the purpose of the Business.

Provided that the indemnity shall not apply in respect of loss of or damage to or any costs or expenses incurred in repairing replacing or making any refund in respect of any defect in such premises

GENERAL EXCEPTIONS TO SECTIONS 1 AND 2

10. The Company will not indemnify the Insured against liability in respect of bodily injury sustained by an Employee and arising out of and in the course of his employment or engagement by the Insured

11. The Company will not indemnify the Insured in respect of

11.1 Any legal liability of whatsoever nature directly or indirectly caused by or contributed to by or arising from

11.1.1. ionising radiations or contamination by radioactivity from any nuclear fuel or from any nuclear waste from the combustion of nuclear fuel

11.1.2. the radioactive toxic explosive or other hazardous properties of any explosive nuclear assembly or nuclear component thereof

11.2 Any consequence whether direct or indirect of war, invasion act of foreign enemy hostilities (whether war be declared or not) civil war rebellion revolution insurrection or military or usurped power

11.3 Injury loss or damage arising out of or in connection with any advice or design specification or professional service given for a fee

SECTION 3 – EMPLOYERS' LIABILITY

12. Insurance Cover

12.1 Indemnity against liability at law for damages and claimants' costs and expenses in respect of bodily injury death or disease sustained by an Employee arising out of and in the course of his employment by the Insured in the business within the Territorial Limits during the Period of Insurance.

12.2 Defence Costs

The Company will pay all costs and expenses incurred with the written consent of the Company in the defence of settlement of any claim covered under clause 12.1.

12.3 Solicitors' Fees

The Company will also pay Solicitors' Fees.

12.4 The indemnity granted by this policy is deemed to be in accordance with the provisions of any law relating to the compulsory insurance of liability to Employees in Great Britain, Northern Ireland, The Channel Islands or The Isle of Man but the Insured shall repay to the Company all sums paid by the Company which the Company would not have been liable to pay but for the provisions of such law.

13. Health and Safety at Work etc Act 1974 – Defence Costs

The Company will subject to the terms exceptions and conditions of this Policy indemnify any Director or Employee of the Insured in respect of

13.1 Legal costs and expenses incurred with the written consent of the Company.

13.2 Legal costs and expenses awarded against a Director or Employee of the Insured.

In connection with the defence of any prosecution (including an appeal against any conviction resulting from a prosecution) as a result of an alleged offence involving injury only to a Director or Employee of the Insured occurring during the Period of Insurance under the Health and Safey at Work Etc Act 1974 or similar safety legislation of Great Britain, Northern Ireland, The Channel Islands or The Isle of Man.

Provided always that

13.3 The Company shall not be liable for the payment of fines or penalties.

13.4 The Company shall not be liable where the prosecution results from a deliberate act or omission.

13.5 Such Director or Employee shall comply with the terms of the Policy.

DEFINITIONS

14. Business

The terms "Business" shall mean the business carried on by the Insured and specified in the Schedule but shall include:

- the provision and management of canteen social sports and welfare organisations for the benefit of Employees
- first aid fire ambulance and security services
- private work carried out by any Employee for the Insured or any director partner or senior official of the Insured

15. Products

The term "Products" shall mean:

- any goods or products (including containers labelling instructions or advice provided therewith) sold supplied erected repaired altered treated or installed in the course of the Business from or in Great Britain, Northern Ireland, the Channel Islands and The Isle of Man.

16. Employee

The term "Employee" shall include:

- any person under a contract of service or apprenticeship with the Insured
- any other person who is borrowed by or hired to the Insured
- any labour master or person supplied by him
- any person supplied by a labour only sub-contractor
- any self-employed person working for the Insured
- any person supplied to the Insured under a contract or agreement the terms of which deem such person to be in the employment of the Insured for the duration of such contract or agreement
- any person engaged under a Work Experience or similar scheme
- any person engaged under the Manpower Commission schemes

17. Insured

The term "Insured" shall include

- under Section 1 – Public Liability and Section 3 – Employers' Liability – any Principal on whose behalf the Insured is undertaking work pursuant to a contract but only for the purpose and to the extent of liability specifically arising under that contract and in respect of Section 3 – Employers' liability only in so far as concerns bodily injury sustained by an Employee of the Insured.
- at the request of the Insured

    any director partner or Employee of the Insured in respect of liability for which the Insured would have been entitled to claim under this insurance if the claim had been made against the Insured any Officer or member of the Insured's canteen social sports or welfare organisations' first aid fire ambulance or security services in his respective capacity as such

- in the event of the death of the Insured any personal representative of the Insured in respect of liability incurred by the Insured.

The term "Insured" shall exclude any Company owned in whole or in part or controlled directly or indirectly by the Insured and which carries on business in the United States of America or Canada.

18. Solicitors' Fees

The term "Solicitors' Fees" shall mean solicitors' fees and other legal costs and expenses incurred with the written consent of the Company for representation of the Insured at

- any coroners' inquest or fatal inquiry arising from any death
- proceedings in any Court of Summary Jurisdiction arising out of any alleged breach of a statutory duty resulting in bodily injury of or loss or damage to property

which may be the subject of a claim under this Policy

19. Territorial Limits

The term "Territorial Limits" shall mean

19.1 in respect of SECTION 1 – PUBLIC LIABILITY

19.1.1. anywhere in Great Britain Northern Ireland the Channel Islands and The Isle of Man

19.1.2 elsewhere in the world in respect of temporary visits by Directors or Employees normally resident in any of the territories specified in **19.1.1.** above but excluding manual work undertaken in the United States of America and/or Canada

19.2 in respect of SECTION 2 – PRODUCTS LIABILITY

anywhere in the world

19.3 in respect of SECTION 3 – EMPLOYERS' LIABILITY

19.3.1 anywhere in Great Britain, Northern Ireland, The Channel Islands and The Isle of Man

19.3.2 elsewhere in the World in respect of temporary visits by Directors or Employees normally resident in any of the territories specified in **19.1.1.** above but excluding manual work undertaken in the United States of America and/or Canada

provided that in respect of injury sustained outside Great Britain, Northern Ireland, The Channel Islands and The Isle of Man the action for damages is brought against the Insured in a Court of Law in such territories.

CONDITIONS

20. INTERPRETATION

20.1 Any word or expression to which a specific meaning has been attached in any part of this Policy or Schedule shall bear such meaning wherever it may appear

20.2 Any dispute concerning the interpretation of the terms conditions and exceptions (or of any phrase or word contained herein) is understood and agreed by both the Insured and the Company to be subject to English law

21. PRECAUTIONS

The Insured shall take and cause to be taken all reasonable precautions to

21.1 prevent bodily injury and loss and damage to property and the sale or supply of any Products which are defective in any way

21.2 comply with all statutory obligations and regulations imposed by any authority

22. ALTERATIONS

The Insured shall give immediate notice to the Company of any alteration which materially affects the risk

23. CLAIMS

23.1 The Insured shall give written notice to Colonia Insurance Company (UK) Limited as soon as possible of

23.1.1. any occurrence or circumstance arising during the Period of Insurance and which may give rise to a claim under this Policy

23.1.2. any claim made or proceedings brought against the Insured or his representative in respect of any occurrence or circumstance referred to in Clause **23.1.1**.

23.2 The Insured shall not admit liability for or negotiate the settlement of any claim without the written consent of the Company which shall be entitled to conduct in the name of the Insured the defence or settlement of any claim and shall have full discretion in the conduct of any proceedings and in the settlement of any claim and the Insured shall give all such information and assistance as the Company may require.

23.2 In connection with any one claim or number of claims other than in respect of claims under Section 3 Employers' Liability occurring in any one Period of Insurance the Company may at any time pay to the Insured the amount of the Limit of Indemnity (after deduction of any damages previously paid to any Claimant or Claimants) or any lesser amount for which such claim or claims can be settled and thereafter the Company shall be under no further liability under this Policy in connection with such claim or claims except for defence costs incurred up to the date of such payment.

24. CROSS LIABILITIES

Where more than one party is named in the Schedule as the Insured and/or the Company is required to indemnify more than one party pursuant to the definition of Insured in Clause 15 cover shall apply as though separate policies had been issued to each such party provided that the liability of the Company to all such parties together shall not exceed in the aggregate the Limit of Idemnity.

25. CANCELLATION

The Company may cancel this Policy by sending thirty days' notice by recorded delivery to the Insured at his last known address and shall return to the Insured the premium less the pro rata portion thereof for the period the policy has been in force subject to adjustment under Clause 26.

26. ADJUSTMENT

If any part of the premium is calculated on estimates the Insured shall within one month from the expiry of each Period of Insurance furnish such details as the Company may require and the premium for such period shall be adjusted subject to any minimum premium.

27. OTHER INSURANCES

If an indemnity is or would but for the existence of this Policy be available to the Insured under any other insurance the Company shall not provide indemnity except in respect of any excess beyond the amount which is or would but for the existence of this Policy be payable under such other insurance.

28. OBSERVANCE

The liability of the Company shall be conditional on the observance by the Insured of the terms and conditions of this Policy and any endorsements thereto.

Reproduced by permission of Colonia Insurance Company (UK) Limited.

APPENDIX E

Association of British Insurers – Statement of General Insurance Practice

The following Statement of normal insurance practice applies to general insurance of policyholders resident in the UK and insured in their private capacity only.

1. **Proposal forms**
   (a) The declaration at the foot of the proposal form should be restricted to completion according to the proposer's knowledge and belief.
   (b) Neither the proposal form nor the policy shall contain any provision converting the statements as to past or present fact in the proposal form into warranties. But insurers may require specific warranties about matters which are material to the risk.
   (c) If not included in the declaration, prominently displayed on the proposal form should be a statement.

   (i) drawing the attention of the proposer to the consequences of the failure to disclose all material facts, explained as those facts an insurer would regard as likely to influence the acceptance and assessment of the proposal;
   (ii) warning that if the proposer is in any doubt about facts considered material, he should disclose them.

   (d) Those matters which insurers have found generally to be material will be the subject of clear questions in proposal forms.
   (e) So far as is practicable, insurers will avoid asking questions which would require expert knowledge beyond that which the proposer could reasonably be expected to possess or obtain or which would require a value judgement on the part of the proposer.
   (f) Unless the prospectus or the proposal form contains full details of the standard cover offered, and whether or not it contains an outline of that cover, the proposal form shall include a prominent statement that a specimen copy of the policy from is available on request.

- (g) Proposal forms shall contain a prominent warning that the proposer should keep a record (including copies of letters) of all information supplied to the insurer for the purpose of entering into the contract.
- (h) The proposal form shall contain a prominent statement that a copy of the completed form:

    - (i) is automatically provided for retention at the time of completion; or
    - (ii) will be supplied as part of the insurer's normal practice; or
    - (iii) will be supplied on request within a period of three months after its completion.

- (i) An insurer shall not raise an issue under the proposal form, unless the policyholder is provided with a copy of the completed form.

2. **Claims**
    - (a) Under the conditions regarding notification of a claim, the policyholder shall not be asked to do more than report a claim and subsequent developments as soon as reasonably possible except in the case of legal processes and claims which a third party requires the policyholder to notify within a fixed time where immediate advice may be required.
    - (b) An insurer will not repudiate liability to indemnify a policyholder:

        - (i) on grounds of non-disclosure of a material fact which a policyholder could not reasonably be expected to have disclosed;
        - (ii) on grounds of misrepresentation unless it is a deliberate or negligent misrepresentation of a material fact;
        - (iii) on grounds of a breach of warranty or condition where the circumstances of the loss are unconnected with the breach unless fraud is involved.

            Paragraph 2 (b) above does not apply to Marine and Aviation policies.

    - (c) Liability under the policy having been established and the amount payable by the insurer agreed, payment will be made without avoidable delay.

3. **Renewal**
    - (a) Renewal notices shall contain a warning about the duty of disclosure including the necessity to advise changes affecting the policy which have occurred since the policy inception or last renewal date, whichever was the later.
    - (b) Renewal notices shall contain a warning that the proposer should keep a record (including copies of letters) of all information supplied to the insurer for the purpose of renewal of the contract.

4. **Commencement**

    Any changes to insurance documents will be made as and when they need to be reprinted, but the Statement will apply in the meantime.

5. Policy documents
Insurers will continue to develop clearer and more explicit proposal forms and policy documents whilst bearing in mind the legal nature of insurance contracts.

6. Disputes
The provisions of the Statement shall be taken into account in arbitration any any other referral procedures which may apply in the event of disputes between policyholders and insurers relating to matters dealt with in the Statement.

7. EEC
This Statement will need reconsideration when the Draft EEC Directive on Insurance Contract Law is adopted and implemented in the United Kingdom.

Reproduced by permission of the Association of British Insurers.

APPENDIX F

List of cases

Bank Voor Handel En Scheepvart NV v Slatford (1952)	2 All ER 956
Banque Financière De La Cité SA v Westgage Insurance Company Limited (1989)	2 All ER 952
Blyth v Birmingham Waterworks Company (1856)	4 WR 204
British Food Freezers Ltd v Industrial Estates Management For Scotland (1977)	Unreported
Carter v Boehm (1766)	3 BURR 1905
Castellain v Preston (1883)	11 QBD 380 CA
Commercial Union Assurance v Hayden (1977)	1 All ER 441
D & F Estates v Church Commissioners for England & Wales (1988)	2 All ER 992
Dearing v Earl of Winchelsea (1787)	
Deyong v Shenburn (1946)	1 All ER 226
Donoghue v Stevenson (1932)	AC 562
Duncan Logan (Contractors) v Royal Exchange Assurance Group (1973)	SLT 192 49–50
Fenton v Thorley (1903)	AC 443 HL
Filliter v Phippard (1847)	11 QBD 347
Forney v Dominion Insurance Co Ltd (1969)	3 All ER 831
Fraser v BN Furman (Productions) (1967)	3 All ER 57
Gale v Motor Union Assurance Co Ltd; Loyst v General Accident Accident Fire & Life (1928)	1KB 359
Gray & Another v Barr (1971)	2 All ER 949
Greenwood v Portwood (1985)	9CL 212
Hair v Prudential Assurance Co Ltd (1983)	2 Lloyd's 667
Harbutts Plasticine Ltd v Wayne Tank & Pump Co Ltd	1 All ER 225
Harrop v Fernandez (1989)	Unreported
Hayler v Chapman (1989)	1 Lloyd's 490
Hedley Byrne & Co Ltd v Heller & Partners Ltd (1963)	2 All ER 575
Hilton v Thomas Burton (Rhodes) (1961)	1 All ER 74
Hooper v Rogers (1974)	3 All ER 417
Horne v Poland & Ors (1922)	2 KB 364

Junior Books v The Veitchi Co Ltd (1982)	3 All ER 201
King v Phillips (1953)	1 All ER 617
Lambert v Cooperative Insurance Society Ltd (1975)	2 Lloyd's 485
Lane (W & J) v Spratt (1970)	1 All ER 162
M/S Aswan Engineering Establishment Company v Iron Trades Insurance Company Limited (1988)	*The Times* July 1988
Mackay v London General Insurance (1935)	51 Ll L Rep 201
McLoughlin v O'Brian & Ors (1982)	2 All ER 298
Mark Rowlands v Berni Inns (1985)	3 All ER 473
Montreal Locomotive Works Ltd v Montreal & AG for Canada (1963)	1 DLR 161
Oxford v Austin (1981)	RTR 416 QBD
Petrofina (UK) Ltd v Magnaload (1983)	3 All ER 33
Poland v John Parr & Sons (1927)	1 KB 236
Post Office v Norwich Union Fire Insurance Society Ltd (1967)	1 All ER 577
Ready Mixed Concrete Ltd v Minister of Pensions & National Insurance (1968)	1 All ER 433
Reynolds & Anderson v Phoenix Assurance Co Ltd	2 Lloyd's 440
Roberts v Plaisted (1989)	2 Lloyd's 341
Rose Lodge v Castle (1966)	2 Lloyd's 113
Rylands v Fletcher (1868)	LR 3 HL 330
Smith (MH) (Plant Hire) v DL Mainwaring (t/as Inshore) (1986)	2 Lloyd's 244
Smith v Stages (1988)	ICR 201
South Staffordshire Tramways v Sickness & Accident Assurance (1891)	1 QB 402
Spartan Steel & Alloys Ltd v Martin & Co (Contractors) Ltd (1972)	3 All ER 557
Stokell v Heywood (1897)	12 TLR 463
Thorman & Ors v New Hampshire Insurance Co (UK) Ltd & Ors (1987)	Unreported
Warren v Henley's Ltd (1948)	2 All ER 955
Wayne Tank & Pump Co Ltd v Employers' Liability Assurance Corporation Ltd (1973)	3 All ER 825
Woolcott v Sun Alliance & London Assurance (1978)	1 All ER 1253
Woolfall & Rimmer Ltd v Moyle (1941)	3 All ER 304
Yewens v Noakes (1880)	6 QBD 530

APPENDIX G

Précis of cases

Carter v Boehm

Utmost good faith (uberrima fides)

This is a very important case which confirmed one of the underlying principles of insurance.

The action was brought by Carter on behalf of his brother, Governor George Carter, against the underwriter, Mr Charles Boehm, in respect of a policy issued on 16 October 1759 to 16 October 1760 for the benefit of the Governor of Fort Marlborough (George Carter) against the loss of Fort Marlborough in the island of Sumatra in the East Indies by it being taken by foreign enemy. The event happened and "the Fort was taken by Count D'Estainge, within the year". The underwriter, Charles Boehm, argued that there had been a fraud by concealment of circumstances which ought to have been disclosed and, in particular, the weakness of the fort and the probability of it being taken by the French.

Part of the evidence in reply to this was that the Governor had £20,000 in effects; and had only insured £10,000 and that he was not guilty of any fault in defending the fort.

It was argued that all the ". . . circumstances were universally known to every merchant upon the exchange of London" and it was further argued by counsel "that the insured is only obliged to discover facts; not ideas or speculations which he may entertain upon such facts".

Evidence was then given regarding the circumstances of correspondence concerning the general warlike activities in the East Indies.

It was held that there had been no concealment or breach of good faith and, during the course of his judgement, Lord Mansfield said:

> Insurance is a contract upon speculation. The special facts, upon which the contingent chance is to be computed, lie most commonly in the knowledge of the insured only: the underwriter trusts to his representation, and proceeds

upon confidence that he does not keep back any circumstance in his knowledge, to mislead the underwriter into a belief that the circumstance does not exist, and to induce him to estimate the risk as if it did not exist.

The keeping back of such circumstance is fraud, and therefore the policy is void. Although the suppression should happen through mistake, without any fraudulent intention; yet still the underwriter is deceived, and the policy is void; because the risk run is really different from the risk understood and intended to be run at the time of the agreement.

The policy would equally be void, against the underwriter, if he concealed; as, if he insured a ship on her voyage, which he privately knew to be arrived: and an action would lie to recover the premium.

. . . Good faith forbids either party from concealing what he privately knows, to draw the other into a bargain, from his ignorance of that fact, and his believing to the contrary.

. . . There are many matters as to which the insured may be innocently silent – he need not mention what the underwriter knows . . . [he] . . . need not mention what the underwriter ought to know; what he takes upon himself the knowledge of; or what he waves [sic] being informed of. The underwriter needs not to be told what lessens the risk agreed and understood to be run by the express terms of the policy. He needs not to be told general topics of speculation; as for instance – the underwriter is bound to know every cause which may occasion natural perils as, the difficulty of the voyage – the kind of seasons – the probability of lightning, hurricanes, earthquakes and etc. He is bound to know every cause which may occasion political perils; from the ruptures of States from war, and the various operations of it.

Castellain v Preston

Indemnity/subrogation

Indemnity is a fundamental principle in all contracts of insurance covering property and legal liabilities and subrogation is a corollary of the principle of indemnity. This case dealt with both of these principles and is one of the most important cases in the development of the law of insurance.

The case was an appeal from a judgement of Chitty J in the Queen's Bench Division whose decision was reversed.

Preston and others owned property including a house which, on 31 July 1878, they contracted to sell to their tenant, Rayner, for £3100 and a deposit was paid. The contract provided that completion should be within two years from the date of the contract.

On 15 August 1878 a fire occurred damaging part of the property and Preston made a claim against the insurers, the London, Liverpool, and Globe Insurance Company. The claim was settled by payment of £330 on 25 March 1878.

On 25 March 1879 Preston named the day for completion as 5 May 1879. The conveyance was completed on 12 December 1879 and the balance of the purchase money was paid.

The action before the court was by Castellain suing on behalf of the insurance company, of which he was an official, who sought to recover the amount paid in settlement of the claim (plus interest) because Preston had sustained no loss as the purchase price had not been reduced by the extent of the fire damage and the money had not been expended on repairs.

During his judgement Brett LJ said:

> The vendors . . . had an insurable interest because they were . . . the legal owners of the property; and because [if the contract was not completed] the vendors, if the house was burnt down, would suffer loss . . .

Earlier, speaking obiter, during the course of the argument by counsel, Lord Justice Brett had said "it may be said that the goods themselves are insured but the assured can recover only to the extent of his interest".

In continuing his judgement he then stated the words which are so often quoted in relation to this case:

> The very foundation, in my opinion, of every rule which has been applied to insurance law is this, namely, that the contract of insurance contained in a marine or fire policy is a contract of indemnity, and of indemnity only, and that

this contract means that the assured in case of a loss which the policy has been made, shall be fully indemnified, but shall never be more than fully indemnified. That is the fundamental principle of insurance and if ever a proposition is brought forward which is at variance with it, that is to say, which either will prevent the assured from obtaining a full indemnity, or which will give to the assured more than full indemnity, that proposition must certainly be wrong.

The learned judge considered the doctrine of notice of abandonment in marine insurance "for the purpose of coming to the doctrine of subrogation". He continued:

That doctrine [of subrogation] does not arise upon any terms of the contract of insurance; it is only another proposition which has been adopted for the purpose of carrying out the fundamental rule which I have mentioned, and it is a doctrine in favour of the underwriters or insurers in order to prevent the assured from recovering more than a full indemnity; it has been adopted solely for that reason. It is not, to my mind, a doctrine applied to insurance law on the ground that underwriters are sureties. They have rights which are sometimes similar to the rights of sureties but that again is in order to prevent the assured from recovering more than a full indemnity . . .

In order to apply the doctrine of subrogation, it seems to me that the full and absolute meaning of the word must be used, that is to say, the insurer must be placed in the position of the assured. Now it seems to me that in order to carry out the fundamental rule of insurance law, this doctrine of subrogation must be carried to the extent which I am now about to endeavour to express, namely, that as between the underwriter and the assured the underwriter is entitled to the advantage of every right of the assured whether such right consists in contract, fulfilled or unfulfilled or in remedy for tort capable of being insisted on, or in any other right, whether by way of condition or otherwise, legal or equitable, which can be, or has been exercised or has accrued, and whether such right could or could not be enforced by the insurer in the name of the assured by the exercise or acquiring of which right or condition the loss against which the assured is insured, can be, or has been diminished. This seems to me to put this doctrine of subrogation in the largest possible form. . .

Much of the judgement then continues with consideration of the contractual arrangements for the sale of the property and the way in which subrogation and indemnity are intertwined.

It was concluded that the insurers were entitled to recover the claim money (and interest) paid to Preston because Preston had sustained no loss in that the purchase monies had not been diminished.

Gale v Motor Union Insurance Company Ltd
Loyst v General Accident Fire and Life Assurance Corporation

Contribution and exclusion clauses

On 4.4.25 Loyst, with Gale's consent, was driving a motor car owned by Gale and he collided with a motor cyclist. In the County Court the motor cyclist recovered damages and costs totalling £154 0s 3d.

At the time of this accident two relevant policies of insurance were in existence. The first in the name of Gale with the Motor Union was in force from 14.8.24 to 13.8.25 in respect of Gale's motor car.

The policy included (*inter alia*) the following words:

> The Company shall indemnify the insured . . . or any relation or friend driving with the insured's consent . . .

The policy contained two conditions immediately relevant to the case.

> Condition 6: The extension of the indemnity to friends or relatives of the insured is conditional upon such friend or relative being a licensed and competent driver and not being insured under any other policy . . .
>
> Condition 10: If at the time of the happening of any accident, injury, damage or loss covered by this policy, there shall be subsisting any other insurance or indemnity of any nature whatsoever covering the same, whether effected by the insured or by any other persons or firm then the company shall not be liable to pay or contribute to any such damage or loss more than a rateable proportion of any sum or sums payable in respect thereof for compensation.

The second policy was in the name Loyst and was with the General Accident and this policy was in force from 31.10.24 to 30.10.25 in respect of the motor car owned by Loyst. So both policies were in force at the time of the accident.

The General Accident policy afforded an indemnity to the insured (Loyst) in respect of his car and further included the words:

> (2) The insured will also be indemnified hereunder whilst personally driving a car not belonging to him provided the insured's own car is not in use at the same time, and provided that there is not other insurance in respect of such car whereby the insured may be indemnified.

There was also a contribution condition in the following terms:

> Condition 5: If at the time of any occurrence of any accident loss or damage there shall be any other indemnity or insurance subsisting whether effected by the insured or by any other person the corporation shall not be liable to pay or

contribute more than a rateable proportion of any sums payable in respect of such accident, loss or damage . . . the due observance and fulfilment of the provisions and conditions of this policy . . . shall be a condition to any liability of the corporation to make any payment under this policy.

In due course Gale claimed against the two insurance companies as trustee for Loyst and Loyst claimed against the two insurance companies on his own behalf. It was argued on their behalf that one or other of the policies covered Loyst and that because of condition 10 of the Motor Union policy and condition 5 of the General Accident policy, the two insurers were liable to contribute rateably. It was argued for the Motor Union that Loyst was insured under another policy and was not covered by their policy. On behalf of General Accident it was contended that the liability of one insurer excluded that of the other.

The arbitrator concluded that Loyst satisfied the requirements of condition 6 of the Motor Union policy and the Company should deal with the claim and that Loyst's claim against the General Accident failed. At the appeal Mr Justice Ross in the course of his judgement said:

The terms of these policies are not so clearly expressed as they might be and have naturally given rise to disputes.

He then continued to discuss the various conditions and said:

Accordingly upon the true construction of these various clauses the assured is not deprived of the indemnity altogether, which would be the result if condition 6 of the Motor Union policy and clause 2 of the General Accident policy stood alone.

He concluded:

In my opinion the proper award in this case is that the claimants should be paid rateably in respect of this accident by the Motor Company and the Accident Corporation. It is agreed that rateably in the circumstances means that each company pays half. I, therefore, direct that each of the respondents shall pay to the claimants the amount awarded by the arbitrator in equal monies.

Harbutts Plasticine Ltd v Wayne Tank and Pump Co Ltd

Indemnity (third party)

The incident which gave rise to this case was considered in Chapter 6 where the case of *Wayne Tank and Pump Co Ltd v Employer's Liability Assurance Corporation Ltd* (1973) was discussed in relation to the policy exception dealing with goods sold and supplied. The above case is also of importance in that the Court of Appeal gave guidance on the correct measure of damages in respect of buildings.

Harbutts owned factory premises at Bathampton in Somerset where it manufactured plasticine. In 1962 Harbutts entered into a contract with Wayne Tank that it should install tanks, pipes and other equipment for the production of plasticine. By early February 1963 the installation work was virtually complete and the equipment was being tested. About 5.30 am on 6th February a serious fire occurred causing extensive damage to buildings, machinery and stock. In fact the building was destroyed.

The losses under Harbutt's insurance policies were agreed at £143,658, including £67,287 in respect of the building. The policies incorporated reinstatement clauses and the loss under the fire policy was settled on a reinstatement basis.

The fire insurers then sought to recover from Wayne Tank within its rights of subrogation. Harbutts contended that the correct measure of damage was the incurred cost of the reinstatement carried out. The court agreed that this was the correct basis upon which Harbutts Plasticine should be paid its claim against Wayne Tank.

Lord Justice Widgery said during the course of his judgement:

> In my opinion each case depends on its own facts, it being remembered, first, that the purpose of the award of damages is to restore the plaintiff to his position before the loss occurred, and secondly, that the plaintiff must act reasonably to mitigate his loss. If the article damaged is a motor car of popular make the plaintiff cannot charge the defendant with the cost of repair when it is cheaper to buy a similar car on the market. On the other hand, if no substitute for the damaged article is available and no reasonable alternative can be provided, the plaintiff should be entitled to the cost of the repair. It was clear in the present case that it was reasonable for the plaintiffs to rebuild their factory, because there was no other way in which they could carry on their business and retain their labour force. The plaintiffs rebuilt their factory to a substantially different design, and if this had involved expenditure beyond the cost of replacing the old, the difference might not

have been recoverable, but there is no suggestion of this here. Nor do I accept that the plaintiffs must give credit under the heading of "betterment" for the fact that their new factory is modern in design and materials. To do so would be the equivalent of forcing the plaintiffs to invest their money in the modernising of their plant which might be highly inconvenient for them.

The judgement also contains the words:

I need only say in this that on the facts of it I consider justice can best be done by awarding the plaintiffs the cost of reinstatement, less any improvement that was not made necessary by the defendant's tort. Even apart from planning and other legal restrictions no man whose plant or building is or are destroyed is bound to reproduce it exactly. He is entitled to act reasonably in using new materials in a new style; but, if he acts unreasonably, or even acts reasonably in allowing himself an improvement, he is not entitled to be paid for his extravagance, even if it were natural for him to take the opportunity to indulge it. The true measure of damage in this case is the actual cost of reasonable reinstatement less the cost of any unnecessary betterment.

Mackay v London General Insurance Co Ltd

Proposal form declaration concealment

Mr H M G C Mackay took out a motor policy with the London General Insurance Co Ltd on 24.9.32. On 5.11.32 he was involved in an accident in which he injured two people and subsequently judgement was given against him for a sum of £830 and costs.

Mackay assumed that this claim and judgement would be dealt with by his insurers but they declined liability on the grounds that he had inaccurately and incorrectly answered questions on the proposal form. One of the questions in the form was: "Has any Offices or Underwriter refused, cancelled or declined to accept or renew such insurance, or required an increased premium or special condition?" Mackay had answered "No" in response to this question.

In fact, some three years before when he was 18 (a minor), he had arranged insurance for a motor cycle with the Ocean Accident and Guarantee Corporation and they had stipulated that they would apply a £2.10s excess clause which was their usual practice with minors. When Mackay had answered "No" to this question on the proposal form he was therefore giving a wrong answer. In giving judgement Mr Justice Swift said "If he had explained the facts I am perfectly certain the insurance would have been accepted – accepted gladly – but as he was so inadvertent to say "No", he has there made an inaccurate statement".

Another question on the proposal form was: "Have you or your driver ever been convicted or had a motor licence endorsed?" Mackay also answered "No" to this question. The fact was, however, that a considerable time before he had been fined a sum of 10s because a nut had become loose on the brakes of his motor cycle and it was said of him that he had been driving this cycle without efficient brakes. In the circumstances, his answer of "No" was inaccurate. At this point of his judgement Mr Justice Swift went on to say:

> I am quite satisfied that both these answers were quite immaterial; that if he had stated the truth in its full detail this insurance company would have jumped at receiving his premium. They would never have dreamed of rejecting his application, but after they have given him the policy, and after the accident has happened and the liability is incurred, they seize upon these inaccuracies in the proposal form in order to repudiate their liability.
>
> I am extremely sorry for the plaintiff in this case. I think he has been very badly treated – shockingly badly treated. They have taken his premium. They have not been in the least bit misled by the answers which he has made . . . but

I cannot help the position. Sorry as I am for him there is nothing I can do to help him. The Law is quite plain . . . here I am quite satisfied that in the circumstances of this case that these answers were quite immaterial, but, unfortunately for the plaintiff by the defendant's form . . . the plaintiff has contracted that the proposal and declaration shall be the basis of the contract between him and the said Company and in the proposal he has made two answers which I cannot say were accurate.

Much as I sympathise with him, I am bound to say that the Company were within their rights when they repudiated their liability under this policy; and I must dismiss this action with costs.

It must be recognised that this case, whilst taking place in 1935, did and does correctly reflect the law about warranties and warranted statements in proposal forms, but reference should be made to the Statement of General Insurance Practice reproduced in Appendix E.

Mark Rowlands v Berni Inns Limited

Landlord/tenant/fire policy/subrogation

Mark Rowlands Limited was the owner of property at 10/12 Lamb Lane and 6/12 Albion Place, Leeds. On 27.1.80 a serious fire occurred at the premises. The fire damage to the building was subsequently agreed at £1,429,166. An action was started by the landlord's insurers (Legal and General), under its rights of subrogation against Berni Inns Limited, the tenant of the part of the building in which the fire had originated. The grounds of the action were negligence/nuisance on the part of Berni Inns Limited as it was agreed that the fire was electrical in origin and that this had arisen because of the fault of Berni Inns Limited.

By way of a counter claim, Berni Inns claimed damages on the grounds that the landlords were in breach of the terms of the lease and it also sought a declaration that the fire insurers were liable to indemnify it (Berni Inns) in respect of the cost of rebuilding and reinstating the premises. In the lease the tenant covenanted:

> to pay the Landlord a sum of . . . money equal to the amount . . . which the Landlord shall . . . expend in effecting . . . the insurance of the demised premises and being a fair proportion . . . of premiums paid in respect of insuring the Landlord's premises in their full rebuilding value . . . including three years back rent of the demised premises . . . against loss or damage by fire . . . and such sum . . . shall be paid to the Landlord on demand on the rent day in each year . . .

This provision was referred to as requiring the tenant to pay an "insurance rent".

The tenant also covenanted to maintain the property ". . . damaged by . . . insured risks excepted . . .".

The landlord covenanted to keep ". . . the demised premises insured against loss or damage by the insured risks and to lay out any monies received under such insurance in rebuilding and reinstating . . .".

The landlord did in fact take out a policy which insured against, *inter alia*, fire and the insurers agreed to pay "the value of the property". The persons named in the policy were Mark Rowlands Limited as mortgagors and the Legal and General as mortgagees; there was no reference to Berni Inns Limited.

A feature in this case is that there had been correspondence between Berni Inns' brokers and Mark Rowlands Limited in the matter of endorsing the name and interest of Berni Inns on the policy. It was suggested that this indicated that the insurance should be for the benefit of the landlord and tenant.

In the lower court it was concluded that:

> ... the true inference to be drawn from the covenants in the lease and from the facts disclosed in the correspondence passing between the defendants and the plaintiffs' insurance brokers ... is that the plaintiffs are to be regarded as having insured the entire premises for the joint benefit of themselves and of the defendants, their tenants ...

The Court of Appeal also considered the question of insurable interest on the part of the tenants, but that is not germaine to the present considerations.

The subrogation action by the insurer against the tenant failed as it was in effect, seeking to recover from its insured.

Several cases were cited but *Mumford Hotels v Wheler* (1963) is particularly interesting as this case deals with the point of the tenant paying the insurance premium and thus having the benefit of the policy.

D & F Estates Ltd and others v Church Commissioners for England and others

Duty of care/economic loss

Wates Ltd (the third defendant) was the main contractor for the construction of a block of flats known as Chelwood House, owned by Church Commissioners for England (the first defendant) and employed a sub-contractor to carry out plastering work on the block.

The plastering was in fact defective and some 15 years after the flats were constructed, Mr and Mrs Tillman, the tenants of one of the flats found that the plaster was loose. An action was commenced by the Tillmans and D & F Estates, the lessee, against the Church Commissioners, as freehold owners and landlords, Hyde Park Property Development Co Ltd, which had employed the main contractor, and the builder Wates, as main contractor.

In the High Court judgement was given for the plaintiffs against Wates in respect of damage caused to the flat by the defective plaster work carried out by sub-contractors employed by Wates.

An appeal by Wates to the Court of Appeal was allowed and the plaintiffs appealed to the House of Lords. Their claim was for the cost of repairs to the plaster and decorations following discovery of defects while the flat was being decorated in August 1980, and for disturbance caused to Mr and Mrs Tillman while repairs were carried out. In addition damages were claimed for the estimated cost of repairs to other defective plaster which had been discovered following an expert investigation in 1983 and for anticipated loss of rent while that defective plaster was being repaired.

The two principal points considered by the House of Lords were, firstly, whether Wates was liable for the negligence of its sub-contractors and, secondly, in the absence of any contractual relationship between the plaintiff and the defendant, whether Wates was liable in tort to the plaintiffs.

The appeal was dismissed and in his judgement Lord Bridge of Harwich made the following comments with regard to these two points:

> It is trite law that the employer of an independent contractor is, in general, not liable for the negligence or other torts committed by the contractor in the course of the execution of the work. To this general rule there are certain well established exceptions or apparent exceptions. Without enumerating them it is sufficient to say that it was accepted by counsel for the plaintiffs that the instant

case could not be accommodated within any of the recognised and established categories by which the exceptions are classified.

His Lordship went on to say:

> If in the course of supervision the main contractor in fact comes to know that the sub-contractor's work is being done in a defective and forseeably dangerous way and if he condones that negligence on the part of the sub-contractor, he will no doubt make himself potentially liable for the consequences of a joint tortfeasor. But the judge made no finding against Wates of actual knowledge and his finding that they "ought to have known" what the manufacturer's instructions were depended on and was vitiated by his earlier misdirection that Wates owed a duty of care to future lessees of Chelwood House in relation to their sub-contractor's work.

On the question of liability in tort Lord Bridge made the following comments:

> It seems to me clear that the cost of replacing the defective plaster itself, either as carried out in 1980 or as intended to be carried out in future, was not an item of damage for which the builder of Chelwood House could possibly be made liable in negligence under the principle of *Donoghue v Stevenson* or any legitimate development of that principle. To make him so liable would be to impose on him for the benefit of those with whom he had no contractual relationship the obligation of one who warranted the quality of the plaster as regards materials, workmanship and fitness for purpose. I am glad to reach the conclusion that this is not the law, if only for the reason that a conclusion to the opposite effect would mean that the courts, in developing the common law, had gone much farther than the legislature were prepared to go in 1972, after comprehensive examination of the subject by the Law Commission, in making builders liable for defects in the quality of their work to all who subsequently acquire interests in buildings they have erected. The statutory duty imposed by the 1972 Act [Defective Premises Act 1972] was confined to dwelling houses and limited to defects appearing within six years. The common law duty, if it existed, could not be so confined or limited. I cannot help feeling that consumer protection is an area of the law where legislation is much better left to legislators.

Lord Bridge also considered the question of what was the defective "thing" as opposed to the "other property" suffering the damage particularly in the case of complex structures such as buildings; the point being that, although the law of tort provides no remedy in respect of repairs to the defective item itself, damages may be awarded for injury or damage caused by the defect. He said that he could not offer any solution to this difficult problem and that any answer would have to depend on the circumstances of the case. However, in the instant case he concluded that:

. . . Wates were under no liability to the plaintiffs for damage attributable to the negligence of their plastering sub-contractor in failing to follow the instructions of the manufacturer of the plaster they were using, but that in any event such damage could not have included the cost of renewing the plaster.

Hair v Prudential Assurance Company Limited

Breach of warranty/non-disclosure/continuing duty

The plaintiff insured a property with the defendants for £8000 and submitted a claim following a serious fire at the property on 5.11.77.

Although this case considered several issues, the point which is of interest in the context of this book relates to the question of whether the insured is under a continuing duty to disclose material facts during the currency of the policy.

The material fact in question was the occupancy of the premises. On the proposal the plaintiff had stated that her son occupied the premises and that the premises would be left unattended for about eight hours daily during weekdays. One of the grounds on which the defendants had repudiated the claim was that the building was unoccupied and uninhabitable and had been left unattended for long periods other than for holidays.

The judge accepted, on the balance of probabilities, that the house had been unoccupied during the months immediately preceding the fire. He did not accept however that the answer given on the proposal amounted to a breach of a continuing obligation in that it required the son to go on living in the premises throughout the period of insurance. If that had been the intention then a specific warranty to that effect should have been incorporated into the policy.

The judge said:

> On this matter I am helpfully referred to the relevant passages in *MacGillvray on Insurance Law* and I will confine myself to drawing attention to the four questions posed at paragraph 754 in determining whether a clause should be construed as a continuing warranty. I bear in mind those considerations. Having done so, it seems to me that the proper way to regard the questions and the answers is to treat them as being an indication of the state of affairs which existed at the time the answers were given, or was going to continue so far as the insured was concerned for the period of the policy but they did not amount to a warranty that no change would occur . . . To regard them as a continuing obligation to have a named individual in occupation throughout the period seems to me to be putting an unreasonable interpretation upon the effect of the questions and answers there appearing.

The four questions referred to at paragraph 754 of *MacGillavray* are as follows:

> In determining whether a clause shall be construed as a continuing warranty the courts have emphasised the following considerations:

(i) does the clause have the appearance of a warranty;
(ii) is it clearly referable to a future situation;
(iii) is it a proposition which would be of little or no value to the insurers if it related only to present facts;
(iv) does a certain breach of the clause permanently prejudice the insurers even if it is subsequently remedied?

Having considered these questions it might reasonably be asked how the judge reached his decision, particularly having regard to (iii), as it seems that the question relating to occupancy would have little, if any, relevance unless it was intended to refer to occupancy of the property during the policy period. However the decision was based on the wording of the particular proposal declaration and the fact that it is up to the insurer to make it absolutely clear if it is intended to be a continuing warranty. Alternatively such a warranty can be incorporated into the insurance contract by an express condition or endorsement on the policy document.

Duncan Logan (Contractors) v Royal Exchange Assurance Group

Insured/reasonable care condition

This case is concerned with a claim by the plaintiffs under a contractors' all risks policy issued to them by the defendants in respect of damage to contract works. The works comprised a temporary bridge which collapsed on 11.11.65 and the defendant declined to indemnify Duncan Logan by relying on a condition of the policy which required that "The Insured shall take all reasonable precautions for the safety of the property . . .".

It is not necessary to detail the exact circumstances which caused the collapse but the insurer argued that the insured was aware that there were defects in the supporting structure of the bridge, such defects having been reported to its maintenance engineer and/or site agent. Despite this, the company had failed to take any action to protect the bridge from collapse. It followed therefore that, as senior employees had known of the problem the insured "knew or ought to have known" of the danger and was therefore in breach of the policy condition.

The court said that although the insured company would be vicariously liable for the negligence of its employees, different conditions applied when it came to construing an insurance policy and it would be wrong to interpret the condition in a way that would mean, in effect, that the insured was undertaking that none of its employees, officers or servants would be negligent or that the condition amounted to a warranty that every employee would take reasonable precautions. The insured in this context is a limited company as represented by the board of directors, and not employees whatever their status. However the company may fail to take reasonable precautions if it employs incompetent officers or fails to take adequate measures or give adequate instructions regarding any danger of which the board of directors were or ought to have been aware.

M/S Aswan Engineering Establishment Co Ltd v Iron Trades Mutual Insurance Co Ltd

Liable at law/goods sold/reasonable precautions

Although the main text refers to this case as giving guidance on the meaning of the words "liable at law" the court also had to consider the reasonable care condition of the policy and an exclusion relating to liability for the cost of replacing or making good sold by the insured.

Between July and September 1980 a company called Lupdine Ltd shipped five consignments of a waterproofing compound known as Lupguard to M/S Aswan Engineering Establishment Co Ltd, a construction company in Kuwait. On arrival in Kuwait the Lupguard was left at the docks and many of the containers collapsed because of the heat, resulting in an extensive loss of Lupguard.

In the subsequent litigation Aswan obtained judgement against Lupdine but the judgement was not satisfied as Lupdine was insolvent. Aswan therefore claimed against Iron Trades under the Third Parties (Rights against Insurers) Act 1930.

Iron Trades contended that it was not liable under the policy for the following reasons:

(a) Under the operative clause of the policy the inclusion of the words "at law" meant that the liability had to be one which arose at common law not under contract.
(b) The nature of the claim came within the terms of exclusion clauses which excluded liability for the cost of replacing, *inter alia*, defective materials and goods.
(c) There had been a breach of condition 3 (the reasonable care condition) in that the defendant was aware of the problem before the fifth consignment and should therefore have taken steps to prevent further loss.

In the High Court Mr Justice Hobhouse held that the claim did come within the terms of the operative clause of the policy and that exclusion clause 5 did not apply. The plaintiff was therefore entitled to recover but the defence relating to breach of condition 3 succeeded with regard to the fifth consignment alone.

The judge's comments with regard to the interpretation of the words "liable at law" are very important as it is submitted that this phrase is synonymous with "legal liability" and one or other of these phrases is at the heart of most liability policies. Iron Trades argued that the words mean liability which arises at common law and not under contract but the policy also included an exclusion in respect of contractual liability. This read:

> This policy shall not apply to liability . . . (6) Assumed under any contract and/or agreement for loss or damage to the contract works and/or materials or plant in use by the insured and/or their subcontractors in connection therewith except in so far as such liability would have attached to the insured in the absence of such contract and/or agreement.

Mr Justice Hobhouse said:

> A policy of this kind needs to be construed having regard to the ordinary use of language. If the words used have an ordinary and natural meaning that is reasonably clear that is the meaning which should be adopted and the Court should not entertain an obscure or contrived argument to give these words some different meaning. This principle is reinforced where it is the insurance company that is seeking to reject the ordinary meaning and where the document is, as here, a standard form document produced by the insurance company itself. "Liable at law" on its ordinary meaning simply means legal lilability . . .
>
> The defendants argued that it was equivalent to liability in tort. But that is not what the wording says. It can be noted that when the defendants wish to refer to such liability they expressly do so a few words later as part of the definition of the second aspect of the basic cover: "liability in tort or under statute . . ."
>
> Their argument was that this was a public liability policy, which it patently is not. The meaning of the relevant words is plain and the first defence must fail.

Referring to the exclusion relating to contractual liability (and other exclusions), which the defendant considered assisted its interpretation of the policy, the judge accepted the plaintiff's argument that this exclusion indicated that there was a basic cover for any liability to a third party even arising from contract. He stated:

> The ordinary meaning of these exclusions contemplated contractual liabilities. It was only by resorting to strained and implausible interpretations of these exclusions that the defendants were able to argue that they could fit them in with their construction of the basic indemnity. In fact they failed to do even that. The presence of these exclusions strongly supports the plaintiff's interpretation of the policy.

Iron Trades also sought to rely on the authority of two Canadian decisions. *The Canadian Indemnity Co Ltd v Andrews, George & Co Ltd* (1950) and *Toronto General Insurance Co Ltd* (1964), but, again, Mr Justice Hobhouse did not consider that these cases gave the insurers any assistance but did in fact demonstrate how an insurance company could exclude contractual liabilities if it wished to do so, as is commonly the case in public liability policies. Turning to the defence based on exclusion 5 which stated:

> This policy shall not apply to liability . . . (5) For the cost of replacing or making good defective materials, plant, machinery, goods or commodities.

The judge said:

> The defendant's submission again depended on putting a strained and unnatural construction on the policy. The liability of Lupdine to Aswan was a liability in damages for the loss of the spilt Lupguard. The damages represented the value of the lost compound. This was not a liability for the cost of replacing or making good anything. What the wording refers to on its natural meaning is a situation where the assured has undertaken a contractual liability to replace or make good as under a guarantee clause in a contract for the sale of goods.

Leaving aside the question of whether this was or was not a public liability policy, it is normal for product liability policies to exclude the cost of replacing or making good the defective product itself and the above comment would seem to be a correct summary of insurers' intentions as regards that specific exclusion. However the question in this case is, "what was the product and was it defective?" The product lost, ie the Lupguard, was not defective, but Mr Justice Hobhouse said that, even if it was accepted that the consignment as a whole (ie product and packaging) was defective:

> . . . it would have been even more clear that the liability of Lupdine was not a liability for the cost of replacing or making good the consignment, it was merely a liability for the value of the spilt Lupguard. These considerations merely demonstrate that the present type of case did not fall within the ambit of exclusion (5) at all.

This interpretation of the exclusion suggests that underwriters may have to consider the wording of their product liability policies as it is surely their intention to exclude the value of the defective product sold whether the claim is one for replacement/repair or merely for reimbursement of the cost of the product.

The third line of defence concerned condition 3 which stated: "The insured shall take reasonable precautions to prevent accidents." It was based on the fact that a Mr Alexander Hamilton, managing director of Lupdine, took no steps to prevent further loss of the fifth consignment after he had become aware of the problem at the docks in Kuwait. On the evidence presented the judge found that Mr Hamilton knew of the problem and deliberately chose to take no steps to deal with it.

Having taken the judgement of Lord Justice Diplock in *Fraser v E N Furman (Productions)* (1967) (see main text) as his authority Mr Justice Hobhouse stated that Mr Hamilton's behaviour had been reckless and that condition 3 therefore applied.

Petrofina (UK) Ltd & Others Magnaload Ltd & Others

Joint insured/subrogation

This case arises out of an accident which occurred whilst construction work was being carried out at an oil refinery. Several parties were involved, each having different interests in the project. Petrofina (UK) Ltd relied on the operation of the refinery for their business and Magnaload was engaged in the installation of a new catalytic cracking unit. The accident occurred during dismantling of lifting equipment used during the installation and it was assumed, for the purpose of the issue before the court, that Magnaload and the second defendants were negligent.

The operator of the refinery claimed under a policy covering the contract works and was paid £1,250,000. The insurers therefore pursued their right of recovery against the defendants. The policy definition of "The Insured" included sub-contractors and Magnaload maintained that the insurer had no right of subrogation because it, Magnaload, being a sub-contractor, was insured under the same policy. The court was therefore asked to consider, as a preliminary issue, whether this was correct and also whether Magnaload was in fact a sub-contractor.

It was held, *inter alia*, that:

(a) Strictly speaking Magnaload was not a sub-contractor but a sub-sub-contractor. It was nevertheless a sub-contractor within the definition in the contracts and within the ordinary meaning of the word "sub-contractors" as contained in the policy. On the true construction of the policy Magnaload and the second defendant were both sub-contractors and both insured under the policy.

(b) Whether the rule that insurers can never sue one co-insured in the name of another is a fundamental principle or whether it rests on the principles of circuity, there is no doubt as to its existence and its application in the case of contractors and sub-contractors engaged in a common enterprise under a building or engineering contract.

McLoughlin v O'Brian and Others

Damages for nervous shock

This was an appeal to the House of Lords by Mrs McLoughlin who had suffered nervous shock as a result of a road accident in which members of her family were involved. The particular significance of the case is that Mrs McLoughlin was not present at the scene of the accident and earlier authorities suggest that damages were not recoverable in a case such as this, on the grounds that the harm suffered was not the reasonably foreseeable result of the defendant's negligence.

As a result of the accident on 19.10.82 Mrs McLoughlin's husband suffered bruising and shock, three of her children were badly injured, and a fourth child was so seriously injured that she died almost immediately.

At the time Mrs McLoughlin was at home and only learned of the accident when it was reported to her over an hour later by someone who had also been involved in the accident. She was told that her husband was dying and that one child had died. At the hospital to which the family had been taken she saw her injured husband and children in circumstances which were very distressing.

At the trial the judge assumed, for the purpose of enabling him to decide the issue of legal liability, that Mrs McLoughlin suffered severe shock, organic depression and a change of personality, as a result of the accident. He held, having reviewed the authorities, that the defendants owed no duty of care to Mrs McLoughlin because the possibility of her suffering injury by nervous shock, in the circumstances, was not reasonably foreseeable.

On appeal to the Court of Appeal the judgement was upheld but not for the same reason. Stephenson LJ took the view that the possibility of injury to the plaintiff by nervous shock was reasonably foreseeable and that the defendants owed the plaintiffs a duty of care. However, he held that the considerations of policy prevented the plaintiff from recovering. Griffiths LJ held that injury by nervous shock was reasonably foreseeable but that no duty of care was owed, and Cumming-Bruce LJ agreed with both judgements.

It was held in the House of Lords that the test for damages for nervous shock was simply reasonable foreseeability of the plaintiff being injured by the defendant's negligent act or omission. Applying this test, the plaintiff was entitled to recover damages because even though

Précis of cases

the plaintiff was not at or near the scene of the accident, either at the time or shortly afterwards, the nervous shock suffered by the plaintiff was a reasonably foreseeable consequence of the defendant's negligence.

It is recommended that the judgements in this case are read in full as they deal with a very difficult, but important, area of the law of negligence, namely when and to whom, a duty of care is owed. The courts have attempted to place limitations on the duty of care and to provide guidelines in answer to these questions. For example, it has been said that to allow recovery of economic loss in the cases of interruption to the public power supply, where there has been no physical damage to the plaintiff's property would "open the floodgates", and, in *Anns v Merton London Borough Council* (1978) Lord Wilberforce proposed a two stage test in order to establish that a duty of care arises in a particular situation. He said:

> First one has to ask whether, as between the alleged wrongdoer and the person who has suffered damage there is a sufficient relationship of proximity or neighbourhood such that, in the reasonable contemplation of the former, carelessness on his part may be likely to cause damage to the latter, in which case a prima facia duty of care arises. Secondly, if the first question is answered affirmatively, it is necessary to consider whether there are any considerations which ought to negative, or to reduce or limit the scope of the duty or the class of persons to whom it is owed or the damages to which a breach of it may give rise.

The second part of the test would seem to contemplate such considerations as the "floodgates" argument and restrictions on the duty of care on account of "public policy".

The two stage test has however been the subject of much judicial criticism recently and in his judgement in the present case Lord Edmund Davies said:

> Was not the action of the appellant in visiting her family in hospital immediately she heard of the accident basically indistinguishable from that of a "rescuer", being intent upon comforting the injured? And was not her action "natural and probable" in the circumstances? I regard the questions as capable only of affirmative answers . . .
>
> I turn to consider the sole basis upon which the Court of Appeal dismissed the claim, that of public policy. They did so on the grounds of what, for short, may be called the "floodgates" argument . . . . My Lord's the experience of a long life in the law have made me very familiar with this "floodgates" argument. I do not, of course, suggest that it can invariably be dismissed as lacking cogency; on the contrary, it has to be weighed carefully, but I have often seen it disproved in later events.

... I remain unconvinced that that the number and area of claims in "shock" cases would be substantially increased or enlarged where the respondents here held liable.

When dealing with the question of policy Lord Edmund-Davies made it clear that he did not consider that the test of foreseeability was the sole basis for determining the extent of liability for the consequences of a negligent act but said that:

... whilst I would have strongly preferred indicating with clarity where the limit of liability should be drawn in such cases as the present, in my judgement the possibility of a wholly new type of policy being raised renders the attainment of such finality unfortunately unattainable. And I think, all we can say is that any invocation of public policy calls for the closest scrutiny. . . .

Rylands v Fletcher

Strict liability

The defendants made a reservoir on land owned by Lord Wilton. Unknown to them the plaintiff had, some years before, undertaken the development of old mineworkings which were connected to other old mine workings beneath Lord Wilton's land. As a result the plaintiff's mine was connected to the mine shafts beneath the reservoir.

Whilst the reservoir was being constructed the shafts were discovered but it was not known or suspected that they had been made for the purpose of getting coal beneath the site of the reservoir. The reservoir, when filled, burst downwards into the shafts and found its way into the plaintiff's mine.

In his judgement, which was approved by the House of Lords, Blackburn J said:

> What is the liability which the law casts upon a person who, like the defendants, lawfully brings on his land something which, though harmless while it remains there, will naturally do mischief if it escape out of his land?

> ... We think that the rule of law is that the person who, for his own purposes, brings on his land, and collects and keeps there anything likely to do mischief if it escapes, must keep it in at his peril, and if he does not do so, he is prima facie answerable for all the damage which is the natural consequence of its escape. He can excuse himself by showing that the escape was owing to the plaintiff's default, or, perhaps that the escape was the consequence of vis major, or the Act of God; but as nothing of this sort exists here, it is unnecessary to enquire what excuse would be sufficient.

This judgement was delivered in the Court of Exchequer Chamber. The case was in fact appealed to the House of Lords where Lord Cairns approved of the judgement of Blackburn J but also emphasised that the defendants had made "non-natural" use of their Land. This has assumed great significance in subsequent cases.

Greenwood v Portwood

Nuisance/tree roots

This case is concerned with the liability of an owner or occupier of land for damage caused to neighbouring property by encroaching tree roots. Liability in such circumstances generally arises under the tort of nuisance and, as indicated in the main text, legal authorities differ on the question of whether liability in nuisance is strict or requires some degree of fault.

Dr Portwood and Mr Greenwood were neighbours and the litigation arose because of damage caused to the latter's property. It was established that the damage was caused as a result of roots from a tree on Dr Portwood's land and also the roots of a hedge owned by the plaintiff, Mr Greenwood, combined with the existence of an underlying clay bed in the ground below the plaintiff's property.

Neither of the parties had any knowledge that the roots had caused, or were likely to cause damage and the plaintiff admitted that he did not expect his neighbour to be any more aware of the problem than he was himself. Furthermore, the judge stated that it would be wrong to attribute to either party knowledge that any risk existed because of the underlying clay bed.

The law governing this situation was explained, and subsequently approved in the Court of Appeal, by the judge in *Solloway v Hampshire County Council* (1981) when he said:

> I therefore find that the law which I have to apply to the facts of the present case to be, that the duty in respect of the nuisance created by the roots arises if the encroachment of those roots is known, or ought to be known, to the owner, occupier or other person responsible for the tree and its maintenance if its encroachment is such as to give rise to a reasonably foreseeable risk that such encroachment will cause damage.

In the case under consideration it was held that the Dr Portwood was not liable in nuisance.

It should be remembered however that the decision was based on the concepts of knowledge and foreseeability and, as time passes, it may well be that the courts would consider that the risk of damage being caused by tree roots had become public knowledge, so that a defendant could not rely on the defence that he or she was unaware of the danger. This would not mean that there had been a change in the underlying legal principles or that the decision in this case had been overruled, but merely that the legal principles had been interpreted in accordance with changed circumstances.

M H Smith (Plant Hire) Ltd v D L Mainwaring (t/as Inshore)

Subrogation

During 1980 MH Smith (Plant Hire) Ltd (the plaintiff) hired a boat from the defendant, DL Mainwaring trading as "Inshore" to transport a dumper across a river in South Wales. The boat sank during the crossing and the dumper was lost.

The plaintiff's insurers settled the claim and, in 1985, it commenced an action against the defendant in the name of its insured. In July 1984 the insurer had obtained an authority from its insured to commence an action in the name of its insured but, unknown to the insurer, MH Smith (Plant Hire) Ltd had been wound up and finally dissolved in March 1985, ie before the proceedings were commenced.

Eventually, when this came to the attention of the insurer, it applied to the Court to substitute itself as plaintiff. In the Swansea High Court it was held that the action could proceed as originally constituted.

Mainwaring appealed and the Court of Appeal held that the action should be struck out. The insurer's right to bring a subrogated claim did not extend to a right to bring a claim in the name of a non-existent plaintiff even where the insurer had taken an assignment to bring an action in the name of its insured.

The position would have been different however if the insurer brought the action in its own name, having obtained a legal assignment of the cause of action from its insured.

The law was summarised in the judgement of Lord Justice O'Connor:

> It has long been the law, where insurers have paid a claim, that they stand in the shoes of the assured in order to recover anything which is relevant to that claim. The law has long been that subrogation entitles the insurers to bring an action in the name of the assured against the wrongdoer to recover anything that is recoverable. The reason for that is that the right of action is vested in the assured. The cases show that an action can be brought by the insurer in its own name where it has taken a legal assignment of the cause of action from the assured. That has not been done in the present case. Thus the insurers were entitled to instruct solicitors to bring this action in the name of their assured as long as the assured existed, but in March 1985, the assured ceased to exist when the company was dissolved. There was no company in whose name any action could be started. In my judgement that has got nothing to do with the right of subrogation. It is a straightforward statement that a non-existent party cannot be party to an action. Nothing in the law of subrogation will save that situation.

Apart from taking a legal assignment of the right of action of the insured, an insurer could escape from this difficulty by applying to the Court for the insured company to be revived under s. 651 of the Companies Act 1985 which provides:

> (1) . . . the court may at any time within 2 years of the date of dissolution, on an application made for the purpose by the liquidator of the company or by any other person appearing to the court to be interested, make an order, on such terms as the court thinks fit, declaring the dissolution to have been void.
> (2) Thereupon such proceedings may be taken as might have been taken if the company had not been dissolved.

Such action was not taken in this case.

Index

absolute liability 5
accidental loss or damage 22–4
accurate description, need for 9
Acts of Parliament 2
  companies 172
  consumer protection 122
  defective premises 55
  employer's liability 45
  energy 68
  and exceptions 45, 52–4, 55, 68
  health and safety 117, 121–2, 128, 131
  law reform 40
  marine insurance 10
  nuclear installations 68
  and policy example 122, 123
  and proviso clause 40
  and recital clause 10, 12, 14
  road traffic 12, 52–4
  and specific cases 172
  and strict liability 5
  third parties 20–1
  unfair contracts 14
  water 5
adjustment 136
  of premiums, notice of 85–6
advice 59
agency 17
alterations 134
Anns v Merton London Borough Council (1978) 167
any one occurrence 36–7
apprenticeship 42–8
"associated" companies 89

Association of British Insurers:
  Statement of General Insurance Practice 14, 137–9

"balance of probabilities" 3
Bank Voor Handel En Scheepvart NV v Slatford (1952) 45, 141
Banque Financière De La Cité SA v Westgage Insurance Company Limited (1989) 11, 141
Blackburn, Justice 169
Blyth v Birmingham Waterworks Company (1856) 3, 141
bodily injury *see* injury
breach of duty 3, 14
breach of warranty 14
  in case example 158–9
Brett, Lord Justice 79, 145–6
Bridge, Lord, of Harwich 155–7
British Food Freezers Ltd v Industrial Estates Management For Scotland (1977) 85, 141
British Insurance Association 5
broker, duty of 16–17
business,
  changes in nature of 29
  definition 131

Cairns, Lord 169
calculation of premiums 86
Canadian Indemnity Co Ltd v Andrews, George & Co Ltd (1950) 162
cancellation 135
  notice of 85–6

care,
    reasonable, in case example   160
    see also duty of care
Carter v Boehm (1883)   11, 141, 143–4
cases,
    list of   141–2
    précis of   143–72
    see also individual cases
Castellain v Preston (1883)   79, 141, 145–6
changes, material, notice of   85
claims,
    "claims made" policy   31–3, 59
    defined   6
    examples of   134–5
    for financial loss   25–8
    investigation, and cooperation   82
    negotiations, conduct in   75–8
    recoverability   11
    Statement of General Insurance Practice on   138
    see also cases
coinsurance   36
Colonia Insurance Company: limited liability policy   1, 125–36
commencement, Statement of General Insurance Practice on   138
Commercial Union Assurance v Hayden (1977)   80, 141
common law   2, 16
Companies Act (1985)   172
"company" in recital clause   9–17
compensation for court attendance   116, 121
compliance with terms and conditions   87
conditions   8, 73–87
    compliance with   87
    examples of   97–9, 112, 123–4, 134–5
    implied   73–4
    precedent   74–5
    subsequent   74
conduct in negotiations claims   75–8
Consumer Protection Act 1987   122
containers   60
contingent motor liability   121, 128–9
continuing duty   14–15
    in case example   158–9

contract,
    law   1–2
    and operative clause   19–33
    of service   42–8
contribution   79–81
    clause in case example   147–8
control of property   91
cooperation and claim investigation   82
costs of legal defence   117, 121–2
cover note   11
cross liabilities   135
    clause   90
Cumming-Bruce, Lord Justice   166
custody of property   91

D & F Estates v Church Commissioners for England & Wales (1988)   28, 141, 155–7
damage   2, 3
    accidental   22–3
    liability in respect to   48–51
    and lifts and escalators   51–5
    location of   62
damages for nervous shock, in case example   166–8
Data Protection Act (1984)   123
Davies, Lord Edmund   167–8
Dearing v Earl of Winchelsea (1787)   80, 141
declaration concealment in proposal form   151–2
defective premises   55, 129
Defective Premises Act (1972)   55
definitions in insurance policy   131–4
Denning, Lord   45, 65
Devlin, Lord   27
Deyong v Shenburn (1946)   51
Diplock, Lord Justice   83–4, 85, 164
directors,
    indemnity to   90–1
    private work for   92
disclosure, duty of   11–14
disputes, Statement of General Insurance Practice on   139
Donaldson, Sir John   32–3
Donoghue v Stevenson (1932)   26, 141
drink   61

Index

Duncan Logan (Contractors) v Royal Exchange Assurance Group (1903)   84, 141, 160
duty,
  breach of   3, 14
  of care   3
    in case example   155–7
  continuing   14–15
    in case example   158–9
  of disclosure   11–14

economic loss   25–9
  in case example   155–7
employees,
  definition   132
  indemnity to   90–1
employers' liability   45, 115, 130–1
Employer's Liability (Defective Equipment) Act 1969   45
endorsements   8
Energy Act 1983   68
European Community,
  on insurance contract law   139
  product liability   62
  and territorial limits   29
exceptions   7
  examples of 96–7, 115, 127–8, 129–30
  relating to uninsurable risks   68
  risks covered by other policies   41–65
    product liability and professional indemnity   57–65
  risks outside scope of policy   67–71
excess clause   68–71
exclusion clause in case example   147–8
executives,
  indemnity to   90–1
  private work for   92
expenses, legal   37–9
extensions to basic policy cover   89–93
  examples of   116, 128–30

faith *see* utmost good faith
fees, solicitors', definition of   133
Fenton v Thorley (1903)   22, 42, 83, 141
Filliter v Phippard (1847)   22, 42, 83, 141
financial loss *see* economic loss

fire policy in case example   153–4
first aid   57
food   61
forms *see* proposal forms
Forney v Dominion Insurance Co Ltd (1969)   69, 141
Fraser v BN Furman (Productions) (1967)   83–4, 141

Gale v Motor Union Assurance Co Ltd: Loyst v General Accident Fire & Life (1928)   81, 141, 147–8
Goddard, Lord Justice   83, 84
good faith *see* utmost good faith
goods,
  in possession   60–1
  repaired or renovated   61–2
  sold or supplied   62–5
    in case example   161–4
  see also product
Gray & Another v Barr (1971)   42, 141
Greenwood v Portwood (1985)   3, 100, 141
Griffiths, Lord Justice   166

Hair v Prudential Assurance Co Ltd (1983)   14, 141, 158–9
Harbutts Plasticine Ltd v Wayne Tank & Pump Co Ltd (1970)   141, 149–50
Harrop v Fernandez (1989)   141
Hayler v Chapman (1989)   71, 76–7, 141
Health and Safety at Work, etc Act (1974)   117, 121–2, 128, 131
Hedley Byrne & Co Ltd v Heller & Partners Ltd (1963)   26–7, 28, 58, 141
Hilton v Thomas Burton (Rhodes) (1961)   48, 141
Hobhouse, Mr Justice 22, 161–4
Hooper v Rogers (1974)   24–5, 141
Horne v Poland & Others (1922)   13, 141

implied conditions   73–4
inclusion of property in insured's custody or control   91
indemnity,
  in case examples   145–6, 149–50
  limit of   35–7, 125–6, 127

indemnity – *continued*
  professional   59
  to directors, executives and
    employees   90–1
independent liability   80–1
injury   2, 3
  accidental   22–3
  and lifts and escalators   51–5
  location of   62
insured,
  in case example   160
  definition   132–3
  in recital clause   9–17
interpretation of conditions   134
investigation, claims, and
    cooperation   82

joint insured clause   89, 165
Junior Books v The Veitchi Co Ltd
    (1982)   27–8, 142

King v Phillips (1953)   23, 142

*Lambert v Cooperative Insurance Society
    Ltd* (1975)   12–13, 14, 142
landlord in case example   153–4
Lane (W & J) v Spratt (1970)   83, 142
late notification   75
law, liable at   161–4
Law Reform Committee   12–13
Law Reform (Miscellaneous Provisions)
    Act 1934   40
legal expenses   37–9
legal liability of tenants   91–2
legal principles   1–8
legislation *see* Acts of Parliament
liability *see* public liability
lifts and escalators, damage, loss or
    injury in   51–5
limit,
  of indemnity   35–7
  of liability   78–9
    policy   125–36
location of injury or damage   62
loss,
  accidental   22–3
  economic or financial   25–9
  in case example   155–7

loss – *continued*
  and lifts and escalators   51–5
  "losses occurring" policy   30
  to property, liability in respect
    to   48–51

*M/S Aswan Engineering Establishment
    Company v Iron Trades Insurance
    Company Limited* (1988)   21–2,
    142, 161–4
Mackay v London General Insurance
    (1935)   14, 142, 151–2
MacKenna, Justice   44
McLoughlin v O'Brian & Others
    (1982)   23, 142, 166–8
Macmillan, Lord   26
Mansfield, Lord   11, 143–4
Marine Insurance Act (1906)   10
Mark Rowlands Ltd v Berni Inns
    (1985)   93, 142, 153–4
material changes, notice of   85
*Montreal Locomotive Works Ltd v Montreal
    & AG for Canada* (1963)   44–5,
    142
Morris, Lord   58
motor liability, contingent   121, 128–9
Mumford Hotels v Wheler (1963)   142,
    154
*Mutual Life Insurance Company of New
    York v Ontario Metal Products
    Company Ltd*   12

nature of risk   11
negligence   2–3
negotiations claims, conduct in   75–8
nervous shock   23
  damages for   166–8
non-disclosure in case example   158–9
notice/notification,
  of cancellation and adjustment of
    premiums   85–6
  late   75
  of material changes   85
Nuclear Installations Act (1965)   68
nuisance   3–4
  in case example   170

observance   136

Index

O'Connor, Lord Justice 171–2
one occurrence, any 36–7
one period 59–60
operative clause 7, 19–33
organisations, sports, social and welfare 92
other policies 136
  see also under exceptions
overseas personal liability 123
Oxford v Austin (1981) 53, 142

pay, liability to 20–2
Pearson Report 5–6
period of insurance 14–15, 29–30
personal liability, overseas 123
personal representatives, indemnity to 40
Petrofina (UK) Ltd v Magnaload (1983) 78, 92, 142, 165
Poland v John Parr & Sons (1927) 47, 142
policy documents 95–9
  Colonia 125–36
  Statement of General Insurance Practice on 139
  Sun Alliance 111–24
possession, goods in 60–1
post accident trauma 24
Post Office v Norwich Union Fire Insurance Society Ltd (1967) 20–1, 142
precautions 134
  reasonable 161–4
précis of cases 143–72
premiums,
  adjustment, notice of 85–6
  calculation 86
private work for directors or senior executives 92
"probabilities, balance of" 3
product,
  definition 132
  liability 60
    examples of 118–21, 127–8
    policy 62–5
  see also goods
professional indemnity 59

property,
  and operative clause 24–5
  see also damage; loss
proposal forms 13–14
  declaration concealment 151–2
  examples of 101–10
  Statement of General Insurance Practice on 137–8
  Sun Alliance Insurance Group 101–10
proviso clause 7, 35–40
public liability,
  policy 95–100
    see also Colonia; Sun Alliance
  see also conditions; exceptions; extensions; legal principles; operative clause; proviso clause; recital clause
Purchas, Lord Justice 17

Ready Mixed Concrete Ltd v Minister of Pensions & National Insurance (1968) 44, 142
reasonable care 82–5
  in case example 160
reasonable precaution in case example 161–4
recital clause 7, 9–17
recoverability of claim 11
refreshments 61
renewal, Statement of General Insurance Practice on 138
renovated goods 61–2
repaired goods 61–2
representatives, personal, indemnity to 40
repudiate, waiver of right to 15–16
Reynolds & Anderson v Phoenix Assurance Co Ltd (1978) 13, 142
right to repudiate, waiver of 15–16
risks,
  uninsurable 68
  see also exceptions
Road Traffic Act 1934 12
Road Traffic Act 1972 53–4
Road Traffic Acts generally 52–3
Roberts v Plaisted (1989) 15–17, 142
Rose Lodge v Castle (1966) 13, 142

Ross, Mr Justice 148
Royal Commission on Civil Liabilities
   (1978) 5–6
Rylands v Fletcher (1868) 4–5, 142, 169

sale of goods 62–5
schedule 8
   examples of 100, 113
Scrutton, Lord Justice 47
service of contract 42–8
shock, nervous 23
*Smith (MH) (Plant Hire) v DL
   Mainwaring (t/as Inshore)*
   (1986) 78, 142, 171–2
Smith v Stages (1988) 47–8, 142
solicitors' fees, definition of 133
Solloway v Hampshire County Council
   (1981) 170
*South Staffordshire Tramways v Sickness &
   Accident Assurance* (1891) 69,
   142
*Spartan Steel & Alloys Ltd v Martin & Co
   (Contractors) Ltd* (1972) 27, 142
sports organisations 92
Statement of General Insurance
   Practice of Association of British
   Insurers 14, 137–9
statements, truth of 87
statutes *see* Acts of Parliament
Stephenson, Lord Justice 166
Stokell v Heywood (1897) 12, 142
strict liability 4–7
   in case example 169
subrogation 76–8
   in case example 145–6, 153–4, 165,
   171–2
subsequent conditions 74
Sun Alliance Insurance Group,
   liability insurance proposal 1,
   101–10
   liability policy 111–24
supply of goods 62–5
Swift, Mr Justice 151–2

Taylor, Lord Justice 78
tenants,
   in case example 153–4
   legal liability 91–2

terms, compliance with 87
territorial limits 29, 92–3
   solicitors' 133–4
Third Parties (Rights Against Insurers)
   Act 1930 20–1
*Thorman & Others v New Hampshire
   Insurance Co (UK) Ltd & Others*
   (1987) 32–3, 142
time *see* period of insurance
Toronto General Insurance Co Ltd
   (1964) 162
torts 2–4
trauma, post accident 24
trespass 4
truth of statements 87

Unfair Contract Terms Act 1977 14
uninsurable risks 68
unsatisfied court judgements 116
utmost good faith 10, 11
   in case example 143–4

waiver of right to repudiate 15–16
warranty breach of 14
   in case example 158–9
Warren v Henley's Ltd (1948) 46–7, 142
Water Act (1984) 5
*Wayne Tank & Pump Co Ltd v Employers'
   Liability Assurance Corporation Ltd*
   (1973) 64–5, 142, 149
welfare organisations 92
Widgery, Lord Justice 149–50
Wilberforce, Lord 167
*Woolcott v Sun Alliance & London
   Assurance* (1978) 13, 142
Woolfall & Rimmer Ltd v Moyle
   (1941) 14–15, 83–4, 85, 142
wording of contract 19–20, 37–8
Wright, Lord 44–5

Yewens v Noakes (1880) 43–4, 142

*Zurich General Accident and Liability
   Insurance Company v
   Morrison* 12